AMERICAN MILITARY PATCH GUIDE

BY

J. L. PETE MORGAN

AND

TED A. THURMAN

AMERICAN MILITARY PATCH GUIDE

BY

J. L. PETE MORGAN AND TED A. THURMAN

Library of Congress Catalog Card Number - 97-070469
Hardcover Edition ISBN - 1-884452-33-7
Softcover Edition ISBN - 1-884452-32-9

Published by:

MOA Press (Medals of America Press)
1929 Fairview Road
Fountain Inn, SC 29644-9137
Telephone: (864) 862-6051
HTTP://WWW.USMEDALS.com
Email: medals @ USMEDALS.com

Printed by Keys Printing
Greenville, South Carolina
United States of America

TABLE OF CONTENTS

ACKNOWLEDGMENTS

The authors wish to recognize and to thank many people for their help in preparing this guide. Among the individuals who have given freely of their time, good advice and support are: COL Frank Foster, Linda Foster, and 1st LT Lee Foster of Medals Of America; Jack McPherson of Lancer Militaria; Don McGrogan; Ira Newman of Action Embroidery Co. And Jim DiRosa of Quartermaster Co.. Special thanks go to Duane Nevins of Battle Dress Unlimited for permitting use of his extensive collection of US Marine Corps patches.

We also deeply appreciate the efforts of COL (Ret) Gerald T. Luchino, Director of the U.S. Army Institute of Heraldry and Mr. Thoms B. Proffitt, Chief, Heraldic Services and Support Division of the U.S. Army Institute Of Heraldry and their staff for their courtesy in reviewing the material for accuracy and content.

And the most sincere thanks to Sara Morgan and Lana Thurman for their encouragement, support, help and patience with Pete and Ted while they spent many long hours assembling, cataloging, collating, scanning and computerizing the entire collection.

Of course, the most praise must go to the people who enjoy and collect patches. This book is for you and we hope that it is some help in increasing your enjoyment and that it will serve not only as a reference source but also as an aid in accumulating and cataloging your collection.

This is the first edition of this work. We hope to have several more. Any errors are the fault of the authors and we apologize in advance. If you have new or different designs that we may incorporate in future editions, or if you would like to discuss anything herein, including sources where to obtain patches for your use, please contact the authors:

J. L. Pete Morgan
5914 E. Cactus Wren Road
Paradise Valley, AZ 85253

Ted A. Thurman
P. O. Box 2361
Prescott, AZ 86302

A Few Words About Patches In General
- And This Book In Particular

While the idea of using a shoulder sleeve insignia to identify a particular unit in the field had its' America start in the civil war, its' U.S. Army rebirth in the twentieth century was not without controversy. The story is told that in October of 1918 in France, the 81st "Wildcat" division began wearing an olive-drab circle with the black representation of a wildcat thereon. The design was to represent that the division had trained at Camp Bragg in North Carolina on the banks of Wildcat Creek. General Pershing felt that this was detrimental to uniform discipline and ordered that the patch be removed. After his staff studied the situation a bit further, it was found that the idea of each unit having a unique design on their uniform had a positive morale effect on the troops, and, trench warfare being what it was in WW I, the army needed all the positive effect it could find.

Being fairly smart (and, after all, he was the Commanding General), Pershing then ordered that all units should design a shoulder sleeve insignia and proceed to wear it on their uniforms. This gave a feeling to the individual that he was a member of a particular group and could take pride in the special accomplishments of that unit. Thus, began the army's headlong rush into insignia design. Soon, every unit had to have their own distinguishing marks on everything from the individual soldier to vehicles, equipment and in some cases, even buildings.

With the advent of WW II and the resulting explosive build-up of the military, shoulder sleeve insignia (SSI) designs proliferated. Hundreds of new designs appeared almost overnight. Designs were coming in from the units themselves, along with professional designs from Hollywood and New York. An entire industry sprang up almost overnight of designers, embroiderers, distributors, and of course, collectors.

The purpose of this book is to provide a military reference source concentrating primarily on U.S. Army designs where most shoulder sleeve insignia originated. However, we have incorporated some of the most popular U.S. Navy and U.S. Marine Corps designs that will be encountered. Keep in mind that in 1947 with the advent of the realignment of the armed services, several major changes occurred. The U.S. Air Force was created and separated from Army control to become an independent entity and the U.S. Marine Corps ceased wearing patches on uniforms.

Future volumes will portray the U.S. Air Force patches. We have included a section in this book to illustrate some of the "Unofficially Authorized" patches prevelant in the U. S. Marine Corps today.

There are many unofficial and variant designs in this book. It is simply because these patches are present today and will undoubtedly be encountered. We have made no distinction between "original" and "reproduction" designs. This is an ongoing debate best left to those who revel in it.

With certain exceptions, the patches pictured in this book are from the author's collection. We hope that you gain as much enjoyment from the hobby as we have. GOOD HUNTING!

PATCH PRODUCTION THROUGH THE YEARS

Methods of construction and material used in making patches have been extremely varied over the years. From the most basic techniques to the highly sophisticated computer operations, the goal has always been to produce a design that someone can wear with pride and purpose.

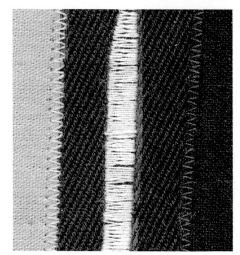

Illustration #1

Originally, appliqués were simply colored bits of cloth sewn together to make a design that met the need. (illustration #1) This led to the designs being embroidered on bits of uniform cloth. First by hand, (Illustration #2) and later, with the development of machines, mass production became the norm.

Early patches were made by machine with the design drawn on the fabric and the maker simply followed the drawing using a single needle. This is a crude method, and takes a skill operator to produce an accurate design. This is commonly seen on in-country made Vietnam era patches (Illustration #3)

Illustration #2

Illustration #3

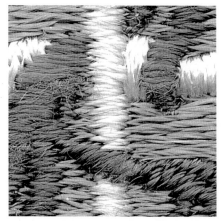

Illustration #4

In the beginning, the most popular fabrics used were usually old bits of uniform on which the design was embroidered. Then, the design was cut out and stitched on the soldier's uniform. The development of the Schiffli machine in the late 19th century permitted the use of bolts or rolls of base fabric with as many as 360 needles embroidering as one. By the time of WWII, the Schiffli stitch had become the standard method by which most all US Military patches were produced. Because the machine was developed in Switzerland, this is sometimes referred to as "Swiss" embroidery. The bobbins are shaped like double-ended boats, hence, the term Schiffli Germi: ("Little Boat"). An example of the schiffli stitch is shown in illustration #4.

Another 19th century invention that was used to produce patches in large volume was the Jacquard weaving machine. This method of weaving was developed in France and employed a series of punched cards which permitted shuttles to move in a predetermined pattern to produce the design. The designs are made ;in one long ribbon and then cut from the strip as needed. This method is commonly used today to make clothing labels, ribbons and fine silk fabrics. A foremost producer of WWII German insignia using this method was the firm Bandfabrik Ewald Vorsteher. Today, in the world of insignia, the "BEVo" is synonymous with this type construction. (Illustration #5)

Illustration #5

With the rise in computer technology, patches are produced today in greater quantity and accuracy than ever before. The small machines can produce from one to twenty pieces at a time using multiple heads which eliminates the necessity of rethreading the needles for color changes. By using computers, it is possible to have registration of color and accuracy of design repeated in every patch in a production run. (Illustration #6)

There are several methods used to finish the edges of patches to prevent the embroidery from unraveling. If the patch is cut from felt, there is normally no finishing and the edges are left raw. In the single needle type, it is common for the stitch to continue around the perimeter of the patch. (Illustration #7) The same is true of hand stitched designs.

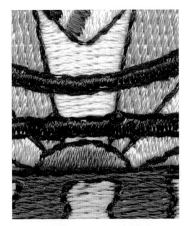

Illustration #6

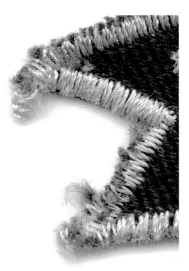

Illustration #7

For schiffli made patches, it is normal for the direction of the perimeter stitch to simply be turned perpendicular to the main body stitch. (Illustration #8) This would in effect lock in the stitches and prevent raveling. The entire patch design would then be cut from the main bolf of fabric and the process was completed. This is called a "cut" edge.

In the 1950's, The Merrowj Sewing Machine Company developed a machine that would make a heavy overlock stitch around the outer perimeter of a patch. This stitch would produce an edge that would not unravel despite rough handling. (Illustration #9) Thisj "merrowing" has become the standard method of finishing edges and is seen on almost all military patches made since the mid-1960's.

Base fabrics upon which the embroidery is done have also changed during the years. Originally, natural fibers were used - cotton, wool, and then linen. This continued until the late 1930s' and the development of man-made fibers. At this point, it became less expensive to use newly developed polyesters or a blend instead of pure natural products. Later, many manufactures came to use a blended polyester base because of the advantages of being colorfast and having minimal shrinkage.

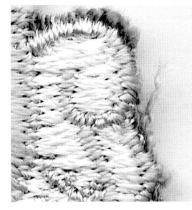

Illustration #8

This is also true of the colored thread used to make the design. In the current market, it is very difficult to find patches being embroidered with anything except a blended polyester threads. Many attempts have been made to try to determine the age of a patch through the types of manufacture, colors of thread used in the bobbin and fiber content. Other tests used are black light, burn tests, smell and taste tests. None of these are absolutely accurate in dating the manufacture of a patch. Collectors should be as knowledgeable as possible regarding the methods of manufacture and construction of patches and made their collecting decision accordingly.

During the Vietnam War, the army changed their field uniform from the familiar OD fatigue uniform that had been standard since WWII to the now familiar Battle Dress Utility (BDU) camouflaged field uniform. On the new uniform, the brightly colored unit patches tended to defeat the camouflage effect desired. It was then decided to make all patches in two fashions. One in the standard colors and another for wear only on the new BDU's. The new patches were in shades of black and olive green in order to blend with the uniform. Although the colors are different, the methods of construction are the same as other patches.

Down through the years since knights painted their crests on their shields to identify themselves to friend and foe alike, man has sought to gain recognition not only as to who they are, but also as to what they are. Thus has come the idea of using colored bits of cloth and metal worn on clothing not only as personal identification but also to indicate the quality of his service in whatever endeavor he has embraced. The shoulder patch is a perfect embodiment of this need. It is little wonder that this small item has proven its value in filling a basic human need. If you are a collector, I hope that you have as much enjoyment as I have had over the last fifty yeas. Happy Collecting!

Illustration #9

How Army Patches & Shoulder Sleeve insignia are worn

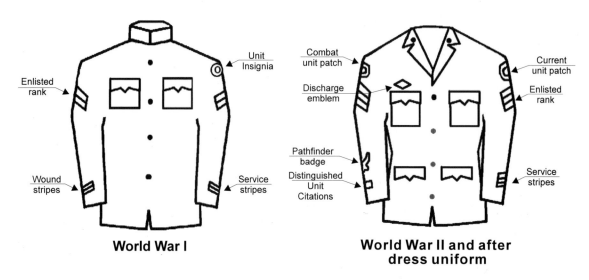

World War I

World War II and after dress uniform

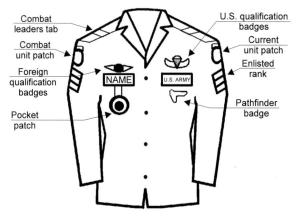

Early Combat Vietnam Era

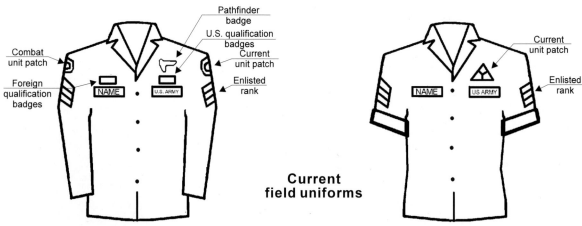

Current field uniforms

NOTE: Some local options may allow wearing of patches elsewhere such as Armor Units patches over the U.S. Army on the left breast.

 ☐ 1st ARMY GROUP

 ☐ 6th ARMY GROUP

 ☐ 12th ARMY GROUP

 ☐ 15th ARMY GROUP

 ☐ 1st ARMY

 ☐ 1st ARMY

 ☐ 1st ARMY (GOLD)

 ☐ 1st ARMY

 ☐ 1st ARMY ARTILLERY

 ☐ 1st ARMY ARTILLERY

 ☐ 1st ARMY AVIATION

 ☐ 1st ARMY ENGINEER HANDMADE

 ☐ 1st ARMY ENGINEER ON WOOL

 ☐ 1st ARMY ENGINEER EMBROIDERED

 ☐ 1st ARMY INFANTRY

 ☐ 1st ARMY MEDICAL

 ☐ 1st ARMY MILITARY POLICE, ON WOOL

 ☐ 1st ARMY MILITARY POLICE, EMBROIDERED

 ☐ 1st ARMY MILITARY POLICE, BOUND EDGE

 ☐ 1st ARMY ORDNANCE

 ☐ 1st ARMY RECON

 ☐ 1st ARMY SIGNAL

 ☐ 1st ARMY QUARTERMASTER, ON WOOL

 ☐ 1st ARMY QUARTERMASTER EMBROIDERED

 ☐ 1st ARMY QUARTERMASTER, BOUND EDGE

 ☐ 1st ARMY, BOUND EDGE

 ☐ 1st ARMY, OG BORDER

 ☐ 1st ALLIED AIRBORNE

 ☐ 2nd ARMY, ON WOOL

 ☐ 2nd ARMY

ARMIES

 2nd ARMY SQUARE

 2nd ARMY, KHAKI

 3rd ARMY

 3rd ARMY, ON BLACK WOOL

 3rd ARMY, ON GREY WOOL

 3rd ARMY SPORTS

 4th ARMY

 5th ARMY (OLD)

 5th ARMY

 5th ARMY AIRBORNE

 6th ARMY (OLD)

 6th ARMY

 HONOR GUARD TAB
6th ARMY

 SEVEN STEPS TO HELL, TAB
7th ARMY

 8th ARMY

 9th ARMY

 10th ARMY

 14th ARMY *

 15th ARMY

CORPS

 I CORPS

 II CORPS

 II CORPS

 II CORPS-RECON

 II CORPS-ARTY

 II CORPS-CAVALRY

 III CORPS

 IV CORPS

 V CORPS-ARTY

 V CORPS

* - WWII Fictitious or Phantom Units

☐ VI CORPS (OLD) ☐ VI CORPS ☐ VI CORPS ☐ VII CORPS (OLD) ☐ VII CORPS ☐ VIII CORPS

☐ IX CORPS ☐ X CORPS (OLD) ☐ X CORPS ☐ XI CORPS (OLD) ☐ XI CORPS ☐ XII CORPS

☐ XIII CORPS ☐ XIV CORPS ☐ XV CORPS (OLD) ☐ XV CORPS ☐ XVI CORPS

☐ XVIII CORPS ☐ XVIII CORPS (COMBAT ASSIGNMENT) ☐ XVIII CORPS (CURRENT ASSIGNMENT) ☐ XIX CORPS (1st DESIGN)

☐ XIX CORPS (2nd DESIGN) ☐ XIX CORPS (3rd DESIGN) ☐ XX CORPS ☐ XXI CORPS ☐ XXII CORPS

☐ XXIII CORPS ☐ XXIV CORPS ☐ XXXI CORPS * ☐ XXXIII CORPS * ☐ XXXVI CORPS

* - WWII Fictitious or Phantom Units

CORPS

☐ 1st ARMORED CORPS

☐ 2nd ARMORED CORPS

☐ 3rd ARMORED CORPS

☐ 4th ARMORED CORPS

☐ 18th ARMORED CORPS

INFANTRY DIVISIONS

☐ 1st DIVISION

☐ 1st DIV. SPORTS

☐ 2nd DIVISION

☐ 3rd DIVISION

☐ 4th DIVISION

☐ 4th DIVISION

☐ 4th DIV. SPORTS

☐ 5th DIVISION (OLD)

☐ 5th DIVISION

☐ HONOR GUARD TAB
☐ 5th DIVISION

* ☐ 6th A/B DIVISION

☐ 7th DIVISION

☐ BAYONET TAB

☐ KOREA TAB
☐ AIRBORNE TAB

☐ 7th DIVISION

☐ 6th DIVISION

☐ 8th DIVISION

☐ 8th A/B DIVISION

☐ 8th A/B DIVISION

* ☐ 9th A/B DIVISION

☐ 9th DIVISION

☐ 9th DIVISION "RIVER RAIDERS"

☐ MOUNTAIN TAB
☐ 10th DIVISION

PAGE 12   * - WWII Fictitious or Phantom Units

 ☐ 10th DIVISION H.Q.

 ☐ 11th DIVISION *

 ☐ 11th A/B DIVISION

 ☐ 11th DIVISION AIR ASSAULT

 ☐ 12th DIVISION (PHILIPPINE)

 ☐ 13th DIVISION

 ☐ 13th A/B DIV.

 ☐ 14th DIVISION

 ☐ 14th DIVISION *

 ☐ 17th DIVISION *

 ☐ 17th A/B DIVISION

 ☐ 18th A/B DIVISION *

 ☐ 19th DIVISION

 ☐ 21st DIVISION *

 ☐ 22nd DIVISION *

 ☐ 23rd DIVISION

 ☐ 24th DIVISION

 ☐ HAWAIIAN DIVISION

 ☐ 25th DIVISION

 ☐ 26th DIVISION ☐

  ☐ 27th DIVISION ☐

 ☐ 28th DIVISION

 ☐ 29th DIVISION

 ☐ 30th DIVISION ☐

 ☐ 31st DIVISION

  ☐ 32nd DIVISION

 ☐ 33rd DIVISION

 ☐ 34th DIVISION

 ☐ 35th DIVISION

☐ 36th DIVISION (OLD)

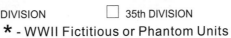 * - WWII Fictitious or Phantom Units

DIVISIONS

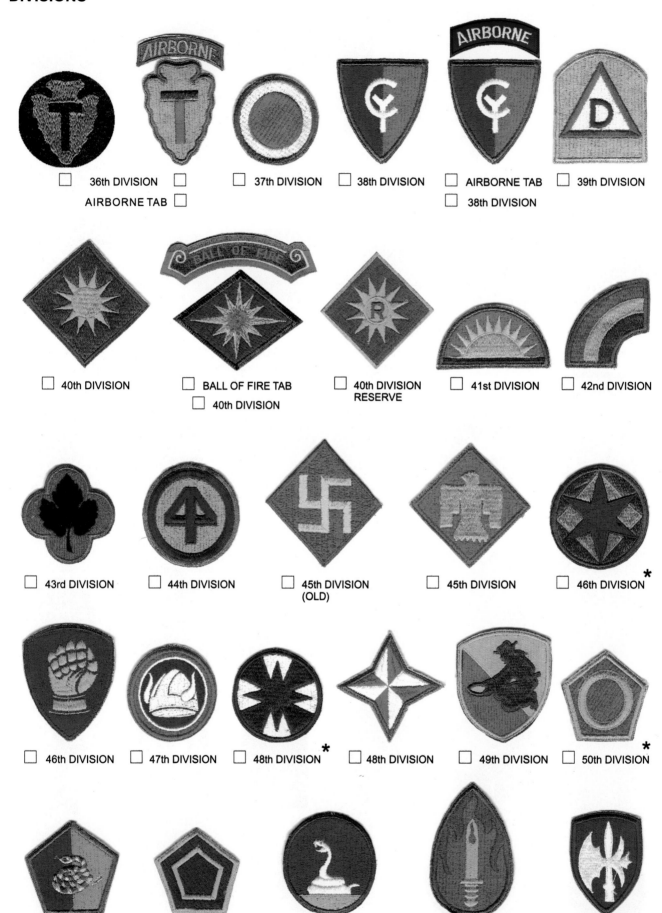

☐ 36th DIVISION ☐   ☐ 37th DIVISION   ☐ 38th DIVISION   ☐ AIRBORNE TAB   ☐ 39th DIVISION

AIRBORNE TAB ☐   ☐ 38th DIVISION

☐ 40th DIVISION   ☐ BALL OF FIRE TAB   ☐ 40th DIVISION   ☐ 41st DIVISION   ☐ 42nd DIVISION

                       ☐ 40th DIVISION   RESERVE

☐ 43rd DIVISION   ☐ 44th DIVISION   ☐ 45th DIVISION   ☐ 45th DIVISION   ☐ 46th DIVISION *

                                               (OLD)

☐ 46th DIVISION   ☐ 47th DIVISION   ☐ 48th DIVISION *   ☐ 48th DIVISION   ☐ 49th DIVISION   ☐ 50th DIVISION *

☐ 51st DIVISION   ☐ 55th DIVISION *   ☐ 59th DIVISION *   ☐ 63rd DIVISION   ☐ 65th DIVISION

✱ - WWII Fictitious or Phantom Units

☐ 66th DIVISION (OLD) ☐

☐ 69th DIVISION

☐ 70th DIVISION

☐ 71st DIVISION

☐ 75th DIVISION

☐ 76th DIVISION

☐ 77th DIVISION (OLD)

☐ 77th DIVISION

☐ 78th DIVISION

☐ 79th DIVISION

☐ 80th DIVISION (OLD)

AIRBORNE TAB ☐

AIRBORNE

☐ 80th DIVISION

AIRBORNE TAB ☐ 80th DIVISION

☐ 81st DIVISION

☐ 82nd A/B DIV.

☐ 83rd DIVISION ☐

☐ 84th DIVISION (OLD)

☐ 84th DIVISION

AIRBORNE

☐ AIRBORNE TAB ☐ 84th DIVISION

☐ 85th DIVISION (OLD)

☐ 85th DIVISION

☐ 86th DIVISION (OLD) ☐

☐ 87th DIVISION

☐ 88th DIVISION (OLD)

☐ 88th DIVISION

☐ 89th DIVISION (OLD)

 ☐ 89th DIVISION

 ☐ 90th DIVISION

 ☐ 91st DIVISION

 ☐ 92nd DIVISION

 ☐ 93rd DIVISION

 ☐ 94th DIVISION

DIVISIONS

☐ 95th DIVISION (OLD)

☐ 95th DIVISION

☐ 95th DIVISION

☐ 96th DIVISION

☐ 97th DIVISION

☐ 98th DIVISION

☐ 99th DIVISION

☐ 100th DIV.

☐ 100th A/B DIV.

☐ 101st A/B DIV. (COMBAT SERVICE)

☐ 101st A/B DIV. (CURRENT ASSIGNMENT)

☐ 102nd DIVISION

☐ 103rd DIVISION

☐ 104th DIVISION

☐ 106th DIVISION

☐ 108th DIVISION *

☐ AIRBORNE TAB *

☐ 108th A/B DIVISION

☐ 119th DIVISION *

☐ 130th DIVISION *

☐ 135th A/B DIVISION *

☐ 141st DIVISION *

☐ 157th DIVISION *

CAVALRY

☐ 1st CAVALRY DIV.

☐ TAB

☐ 1st CAVALRY EXPERT

☐ TAB

☐ 1st CAVALRY AIRMOBILE

☐ 1st CAVALRY A/B

* - WWII Fictitious or Phantom Units

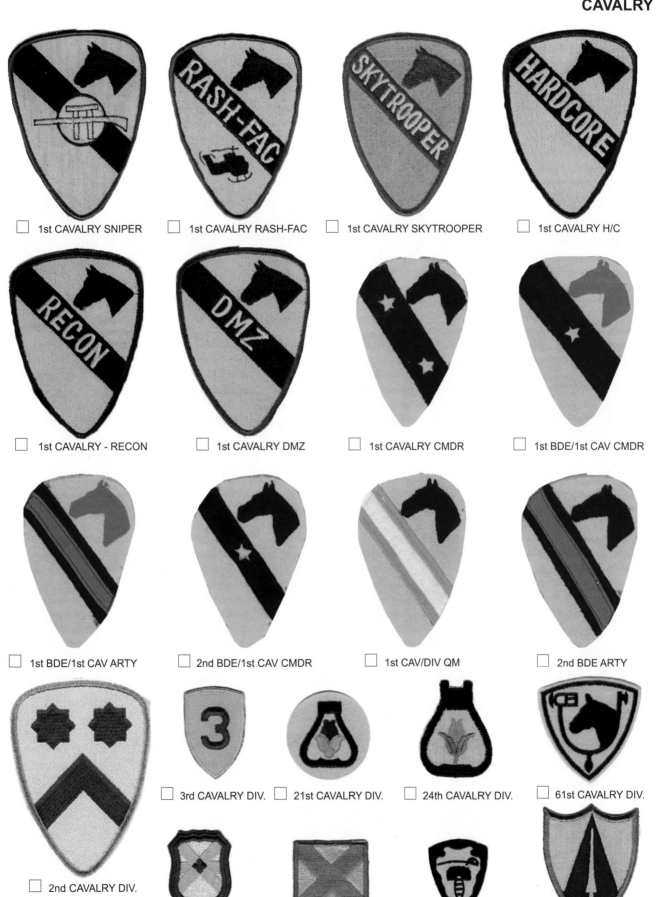

☐ 1st CAVALRY SNIPER ☐ 1st CAVALRY RASH-FAC ☐ 1st CAVALRY SKYTROOPER ☐ 1st CAVALRY H/C

☐ 1st CAVALRY - RECON ☐ 1st CAVALRY DMZ ☐ 1st CAVALRY CMDR ☐ 1st BDE/1st CAV CMDR

☐ 1st BDE/1st CAV ARTY ☐ 2nd BDE/1st CAV CMDR ☐ 1st CAV/DIV QM ☐ 2nd BDE ARTY

☐ 3rd CAVALRY DIV. ☐ 21st CAVALRY DIV. ☐ 24th CAVALRY DIV. ☐ 61st CAVALRY DIV.

☐ 2nd CAVALRY DIV.

☐ 62nd CAVALRY DIV. ☐ 63rd CAVALRY DIV. ☐ 64th CAVALRY DIV. ☐ 65th CAVALRY DIV.

CAVALRY

☐ 66th CAVALRY DIVISION

☐ 6th CAVALRY BRIGADE

☐ 1st CAVALRY REGT.(MECH)

☐ 7th CAVALRY REGT. (MECH)

☐ 13th CAVALRY REGT.(MECH)

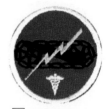

☐ 4th MEDICAL TROOP

☐ 19th ORDNANCE TROOP

☐ 47th ENGR SQDN.

☐ 13th QM CO.

☐ 68th FIELD ARTY BN.(MECH)

☐ 68th FIELD ARTY BN.(MECH)

☐ 56th CAVALRY BRIGADE

☐ 6th CAVALRY GRP.

☐ 1st CAV DIV. HAT PATCH

☐ 1st CAV REGT.

☐ 1st CAVALRY SECURITY POLICE

☐ 4th CAVALRY REGT.

☐ 6th CAVALRY REGT.

☐ 7th CAVALRY REGT.

☐ 7th CAVALRY REGT.

☐ 8th CAVALRY REGIMENT

☐ 8th RECON CO.

☐ 9th CAV REGT.

☐ AERO SCOUTS

☐ 10th CAV REGT.

☐ 10th CAV REGT KOREA

☐ 10th CAV REGT 7th DIVISION

☐ 12th CAVALRY REGIMENT

☐ 15th CAVALRY REGIMENT

☐ 17th CAVALRY REGIMENT

☐ 93rd RECON BN.

☐ 107th CAV REGT

ARMORED CAVALRY REGIMENTS

- [ ] 2nd ACR
- [ ] 3rd ACR
- [ ] 3rd ACR " DESERT STORM"
- [ ] 6th ACR
- [ ] 11th ACR

- [ ] 14th ACR
- [ ] 16th ACR "TROOP C"
- [ ] 32nd ACR
- [ ] 104th ACR
- [ ] 104th ARM/CAV REGT. "GOVERNOR'S TROOP"

- [ ] 107th ACR
- [ ] 108th ACR
- [ ] 112th ARMORED CAVALRY REGIMENT
- [ ] 116th ACR
- [ ] 163rd ACR

ARMORED UNITS

- [ ] U.S. ARMORED FORCE

TABS
- [ ]
- [ ]
- [ ]
- [ ]

- [ ] ARMORED FORCES SCHOOL

TABS
- [ ]
- [ ]

- [ ] 1st ARMD DIV.

- [ ] 2nd ARMD DIV.
- [ ] TAB

- [ ] 3rd ARMD DIV.
- [ ] TAB

- [ ] 3rd ARMD RECON BN.

TABS
- [ ]
- [ ]

- [ ] 4th ARMD DIV.

- [ ] 4th ARMD DIV. MARKSMANSHIP

- [ ] 5th ARMD DIV.
- [ ] TAB

PAGE 19

ARMORED

6 SUPER SIXTH
- [ ] 6th ARMD DIV.
- [ ] TAB

7 THE LUCKY "7TH"
- [ ] 7th ARMD DIV.
- [ ] TAB

TABS
- [ ]
- [ ]
- [ ]

8 IRON SNAKE / THUNDERING HERD / IRON DEUCE
- [ ] 8th ARMD DIV.

TABS
- [ ]
- [ ]

9 PHANTOM / REMAGEN
- [ ] 9th ARMD DIV.

10 TIGER
- [ ] 10th ARMD DIV.
- [ ] TAB

- [ ] 10th ARMORED DIVISION

11 THUNDERBOLT
- [ ] 11th ARMD DIV.
- [ ] TAB

12 HELL CAT
- [ ] 12th ARMD DIV.
- [ ] TAB

- [ ] 12th ARMORED DIVISION

13 BLACK CAT
- [ ] 13th ARMD DIV.
- [ ] TAB

14 LIBERATOR
- [ ] 14th ARMD DIV.
- [ ] TAB

- [ ] 14th ARMD DIV.

15
- [ ] 15th ARMD DIV.

16
- [ ] 16th ARMD DIV.

17
- [ ] 17th ARMD DIV.

18
- [ ] 18th ARMD DIV.

19
- [ ] 19th ARMD DIV.

20
- [ ] 20th ARMD DIV.

21
- [ ] 21st ARMD DIV.

22
- [ ] 22nd ARMD DIV.

23
- [ ] 23rd ARMD DIV.

27 EMPIRE
- [ ] 27th ARMD DIV.
- [ ] TAB

28
- [ ] 28th ARMD DIV.

30 VOLUNTEERS
- [ ] 30th ARMD DIV.
- [ ] TAB

40 GRIZZLY
- [ ] 40th ARMD DIV.
- [ ] TAB

48 HURRICANE
- [ ] 48th ARMD DIV.
- [ ] TAB

49 LONE ☆ STAR
- [ ] 49th ARMD DIV.
- [ ] TAB

50 JERSEY BLUES
- [ ] 50th ARMD DIV.
- [ ] TAB

16 GP
- [ ] 16th ARMD GROUP

17 GP
- [ ] 17th ARMD GROUP

☐ 1st TANK BN/72nd ARMOR ☐ SMC ☐ 7th ARMY TANK TRAINING CENTER ☐ DEMONSTRATION REGT. ☐ HEADQUARTERS ARMORED FORCES

☐ GENERAL HQ ☐ ARMOR SCHOOL ☐ ARMORED FORCES ☐ TANKER DIAMOND

☐ TANK DESTROYER FORCES ☐ 3/16th ARMOR ☐ 2/103rd ARMOR ☐ 1/110th ARMOR ☐ 2/196th ARMOR

☐ 306th TANK BN. ☐ 710th TANK BN. ☐ 714th TANK BN. ☐ 2nd ARMOR ☐ 34th ARMOR

☐ 42nd TANK BN ☐ 44th TANK BN ☐ 72nd ARMOR ☐ 73rd ARMOR ☐ 77th ARMOR ☐ 79th TANK BN.

☐ 81st ARMOR ☐ 131st ARMOR ☐ 142nd ARMOR ☐ 714th TANK BN ☐ 715th TANK BN. ☐ 826th TANK BN.

☐ ARMY GROUND FORCES

☐ ARMY SERVICE FORCES

☐ REPLACEMENT & SCHOOL CMD.

☐ ARMY GROUND FORCES REPLACEMENT DEPOTS

☐ GROUND H.Q. RESERVE

☐ 1st SERVICE CMD.

☐ 2nd SERVICE CMD.

☐ 3rd SERVICE CMD.

☐ 4th SERVICE CMD.

☐ 5th SERVICE CMD.

☐ 5th SERVICE CMD.

☐ 6th SERVICE CMD.

☐ 7th SERVICE CMD.

☐ 7th SERVICE CMD.

☐ 7th SERVICE CMD. CAMP CROWDER

☐ 8th SERVICE CMD.

☐ 9th SERVICE CMD.

☐ NORTHWEST SERVICE CMD.

☐ ASF TRAINING CENTER

☐ ANTI-AIRCRAFT CMD.

☐ ANTI-AIRCRAFT CMD. (EASTERN)

☐ ANTI-AIRCRAFT CMD. (CENTRAL)

☐ ANTI-AIRCRAFT CMD. (SOUTHERN)

☐ DEFENSE CMD. (WESTERN)

☐ DEFENSE CMD. (EASTERN)

☐ DEFENSE CMD. (SOUTHERN)

☐ 1st COAST ARTILLERY

☐ 2nd COAST ARTILLERY

☐ 3rd COAST ARTILLERY

☐ 4th COAST ARTILLERY

☐ 9th COAST ARTY.   ☐ HAWAIIAN COASTAL DEFENSE   ☐ HAWAIIAN COAST ARTILLERY BDE.   ☐ MILITARY DISTRICT OF WASHINGTON   ☐ MILITARY DISTRICT OF WASHINGTON, H.Q. CO.

☐ AIRBORNE CMD.   ☐ PORTS OF EMBARKATION   ☐ OCS   ☐ RANGER BATTALIONS   ☐ MILITARY PERSONNEL VETERANS ADMIN.

☐ ARMY AMPHIBIAN UNITS   ☐ ARMY SPECIALIZED TRAINING PROGRAM   ☐ ARMY SPECIALIZED TRAINING PROGRAM RESERVE   ☐ ENGINEER SPECIAL BRIGADES   ☐ CARIBBEAN DEFENSE COMMAND

☐ GUAM COMMAND   ☐ CHINA, BURMA, INDIA THEATER   ☐ BERMUDA BASE COMMAND   ☐ U.S. ARMY PACIFIC   ☐ PHILIPPINE DEPT.   ☐ ALASKAN DEFENSE COMMAND

☐ BONIN, GUAM, MARIANNAS COMMAND   ☐ HAWAIIAN DEPT.   ☐ ANTILLES DEPT.   ☐ SOUTH ATLANTIC FORCES   ☐ ALEUTIAN ISLANDS COMMAND

☐ ATLANTIC BASE CMD.   ☐ ICELAND BASE CMD.   ☐ LABRADOR, N.E. CANADA BASE CMD.   ☐ GREENLAND BASE COMMAND

GROUND UNITS

 ☐ ALASKAN DEF. COMMAND

 ☐ ALASKAN COMM. SYSTEM

 ☐ GENERAL HQ SW PACIFIC

 ☐ KISKA TASK FORCE

 ☐ U.S. ARMY FORCES WESTERN PACIFIC

 ☐ PANAMA HELLGATE

 ☐ PANAMA CANAL DEPT.

 ☐ S.E. ASIA COMMAND

 ☐ KOREAN MIL. ASSISTANCE GRP.
☐ TAB

 ☐ MILITARY GOV. OF KOREA

 ☐ KOREAN CMD ZONE

 ☐ RYUKYUS COMMAND

 ☐ RYUKUS COMMAND

 ☐ U.S. FORCES FAR EAST

 ☐ 8231st ARMY UNIT SPECIAL OPERATIONS DETACHMENT

 ☐ JOINT FAR EAST CMD., HQ

 ☐ US FORCES FAR EAST A/B PATHFINDER

 ☐ JAPAN MILITARY TRIALS STAFF

 ☐ MILITARY INTELLIGENCE JAPAN OCCUPATION

 ☐ CHINA COMBAT TRAINING CMD.

 ☐ CHINA, HQ

 ☐ LEDO ROAD

 ☐ PHILIPPINE GENERAL STAFF

 ☐ NORTH AFRICAN THEATER

 ☐ U.S. ARMY FORCES MIDDLE EAST

 ☐ PERSIAN GULF COMMAND

TAB ☐

 ☐ SUPREME HQ ALLIED EXPEDITIONARY FORCES (SHAEF)

 ☐ ALLIED FORCES HEADQUARTERS

 ☐ ALLIED FORCES HEADQUARTERS

☐ HEADQUARTERS
EUROPEAN THEATER
OF OPERATIONS

☐ EUROPEAN THEATER
OF OPERATIONS
ADVANCED BASE

☐ EUROPEAN THEATER
OF OPERATIONS

☐ EUROPEAN
COMMAND
ZONE

☐ U.S. ARMY
EUROPE

☐ LONDON BASE
COMMAND

☐ EUROPEAN
CONSTABULARY

☐ EUROPEAN
CIVIL AFFAIRS

☐ US ARMY
EUROPE A/B

☐ US ARMY
FRANKFURT

☐ US ARMY
BERLIN

☐ BERLIN DISTRICT

☐ NUREMBERG
DISTRICT

TAB
☐

☐ AUSTRIAN OCCUPATION
FORCES

☐ AUSTRIAN
TACTICAL
COMMAND

☐ ALLIED CONTROL
COMMISSION-HUNGARY

☐ MISSION TO
MOSCOW

☐ USMLM-POTSDAM

☐ ALLIED CONTROL
COMMISSION
BULGARIA

TAB
☐

☐ US FORCES IN
TRIESTE

☐ MISSION TO
IRAN

☐ MISSION TO IRAN

☐ MISSION TO
SAUDI ARABIA

☐ UNITED NATIONS

☐ UNITED NATIONS
HEADQUARTERS

☐ QUARTERMASTER
CORPS

GROUND UNITS

☐ RECRUITING
SERVICE

☐ RECRUITING
SERVICE

☐ RECRUITING
SERVICE

RECRUITING TABS

RECRUITING TABS

☐ FIRST ARMY ☐ SECOND ARMY ☐ THIRD ARMY ☐ FOURTH ARMY

☐ FIFTH ARMY ☐ SIXTH ARMY ☐ ALASKA ☐ HAWAII

☐ RECRUITING SERVICE

☐ TRANSPORTATION
CORPS

☐ 'RED BALL EXPRESS'
TRANSPORTATION
CORPS

☐ SIGNAL CORPS

☐ 1st FILIPINO UNIT

☐ AVIATION ENGINEERS

☐ AVIATION ENGINEERS

☐ KACHIN RANGERS

☐ JINGPAW RANGERS

☐ 1st SPECIAL
SERVICE GRP.

☐ (O.S.S.) OFFICE OF
STRATEGIC SERVICES

☐ SPECIAL ALLIED A/B
RECON FORCE, O.S.S.

☐ SPECIAL CATEGORY
ARMY WITH AIR FORCE
(SCARFWAF)

☐ 5307th COMPOSITE UNIT
"MERRILL'S MARAUDERS"

☐ SPECIAL FORCE, O.S.S.

☐ 5307th COMPOSITE UNIT
"MERRILL'S MARAUDERS"

☐ COMBINED OPERATIONS

☐ ANTI-AIRCRAFT
ARTY. (AAA) SCH.

☐ 14th AAA COMMAND

☐ 99th BN. COMBAT TEAM

☐ 99th INFANTRY BN

☐ 480th FIELD ARTILLERY BN.

☐ BOMB DISPOSAL PERSONNEL

☐ TASK FORCE

☐ FRANCE WAR AID

☐ FRANCE WAR AID

☐ EMBASSY GUARD

CHEMICAL UNITS

☐ US ARMY CHEMICAL CORPS

☐ CHEMICAL CORPS

☐ 2nd CHEMICAL MORTAR BN.

☐ 81st CHEMICAL MORTAR BN

☐ 84th CHEMICAL MORTAR BN.

☐ 83rd CHEMICAL MORTAR BN.

☐ 91st CHEMICAL MORTAR BN.

☐ 93rd CHEMICAL MORTAR BN.

☐ 93rd CHEMICAL MORTAR BDE.

☐ 96th CHEMICAL MORTAR BN.

☐ 460th CHEMICAL BDE.

☐ 464th CHEMICAL BDE.

☐ 415th CHEMICAL BDE.

REGIMENTAL COMBAT TEAMS

☐ 4th R.C.T

☐ 5th R.C.T.

☐ 5th R.C.T.

☐ 5th R.C.T.

☐ 25th R.C.T.

☐ 29th R.C.T.

REGIMENTAL COMBAT TEAMS (R.C.T.)

☐ 33rd R.C.T.

☐ 38th R.C.T.

☐ 65th R.C.T.

☐ 74th R.C.T.

☐ 74th R.C.T. (ERROR)

☐ 75th R.C.T.

☐ 103rd R.C.T.

☐ 107th R.C.T.

☐ 111th R.C.T.

☐ 150th R.C.T.

☐ 157th R.C.T.

☐ 158th R.C.T.

☐ 163rd R.C.T.

☐ 166th R.C.T.

☐ 176th R.C.T.

☐ 178th R.C.T.

☐ 182nd R.C.T.

☐ 187th R.C.T.

☐ 196th R.C.T.

☐ 278th R.C.T.

☐ 295th R.C.T.

☐ 296th R.C.T.

☐ 298th R.C.T.

☐ 299th R.C.T.

☐ 351st R.C.T.

☐ 442nd R.C.T. (OLD)

☐ 442nd R.C.T.

☐ 508th R.C.T.

☐ U.S. PARATROOPS

☐ A/B BOARD HALO PARACHUTIST

☐ AIRBORNE ORIENTATION

☐ A/B INSTRUCTOR

☐ 18th A/B CORPS ARTILLERY

☐ 82nd AIRBORNE HEADQUARTERS

☐ 82nd A/B ARTY. BN.

☐ 152nd A/B ARTILLERY

☐ 173rd A/B BDE., SNIPER

☐ 187th A/B INFANTRY REGIMENT

☐ 187th A/B R.C.T.

☐ 187th A/B INF. RGT.

☐ 187th A/B INF. RGT.

☐ 187th A/B PARAGLIDER INF. RGT.

☐ 187th A/B R.C.T.

☐ 187th A/B INF. MORTAR BAT.

☐ 188th A/B INF. RGT.

☐ 188th A/B INF. RGT.

☐ 188th A/B INF. RGT.

☐ 325th A/B INF. RGT.

☐ 325th A/B INF. RGT.

☐ 325th A/B INF. RGT.

☐ 501st A/B INF. RGT.

☐ 502nd A/B INF. RGT.

☐ 502nd A/B INF. RGT.

☐ 503rd A/B INF. RGT.

☐ 377th A/B ARTY.

AIRBORNE UNITS

☐ 503rd A/B
INF. RGT.

☐ 503rd PARAMARINE

☐ 503rd A/B
INF. RGT.

☐ 504th A/B
INF. RGT.

☐ 504th A/BINF.
RGT., H&H

☐ 504th A/B INF.
RGT., "E" CO.

☐ 504th A/B INF.
RGT., "A" CO.

☐ 504th A/B
INF. RGT.

☐ 505th A/B
INF. RGT.

☐ 505th A/B
INF. RGT.

☐ 505th A/B
INF. RGT.

☐ 505th A/B
INF. RGT.

☐ 506th A/B
INF. RGT.

☐ 507th A/B INF. RGT.

☐ 508th A/B INF. RGT.

☐ 508th A/B INF. RGT.

☐ 508th A/B
INF. RGT.

☐ 509th A/B
INF. RGT.

☐ 509th A/B INF.
RGT., 2nd BN.

☐ 511th A/B
INF. RGT.

☐ 511th A/B
INF. RGT.

☐ 511th A/B
INF. RGT.

☐ 513th A/B INF.
REGIMENT

☐ 513th A/B
INF. RGT.

☐ 515th A/B INF. RGT.

☐ 517th A/B
INF. RGT.

☐ 517th A/B INF. RGT.

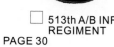

☐ 541st A/B INFANTRY REGIMENT

☐ 542nd A/B INFANTRY BATTALION

☐ 550th A/B INFANTRY BATTALION

☐ 551st A/B INFANTRY BATTALION

☐ 101st A/B DIV. SUPPORT CMD.

☐ 127th A/B ENGR. BATTALION

☐ 307th A/B ENGR. BATTALION

☐ 462nd A/B FIELD ARTILLERY BN.

☐ A/B PARACHUTE RIGGER

☐ 82nd A/B DIV. CMD. & CONTROL

☐ 82nd A/B DIV. SUPPORT CMD.

☐ 82nd A/B DIVISION SIGNAL BN.

☐ 674th A/B FIELD ARTILLERY BN.

☐ A/B AERIAL SUPPLY

☐ AERIAL SUPPLY

☐ A/B PATHFINDER

☐ GLIDER TROOPS

☐ U.S. ARMY PARACHUTE TEAM

☐ U.S. ARMY PARACHUTE TEAM

☐ 1st INFANTRY DIVISION

☐ 2nd INF. DIV., IMJIN SCOUTS

☐ 3rd INFANTRY REGIMENT

☐ 3rd INFANTRY REGIMENT

☐ 4th INFANTRY REGIMENT PAGE 31

INFANTRY UNITS

☐ 4th INFANTRY DIV.,
DISCOM PATROL

☐ 6th INF. REGIMENT,
1st BN; "D" CO.

☐ 6th INFANTRY
REGIMENT

☐ 7th INFANTRY
REGIMENT

☐ 8th INFANTRY
REGIMENT

☐ 9th INFANTRY
REGIMENT

☐ 9th INF. REGIMENT,
6th BN.

☐ 10th INF. REGT.,
1st BN.

☐ 11th INF.
REGIMENT

☐ 12th INF.
REGIMENT

☐ 12th INF. RGT.,
1st BN., "A" CO.

☐ 13th INF.
RGT.

☐ 14th INF.
RGT.

☐ 15th INFANTRY
REGIMENT

☐ 16th INFANTRY
REGIMENT

☐ 17th INF. RGT.,
7th DIV.

☐ 18th INFANTRY
REGIMENT

☐ 20th INF.
REGIMENT

☐ 21st INFANTRY
REGIMENT

☐ 21st INFANTRY RGT.
'GIMLET GRENADIERS'

☐ 22nd INF.
RGT.

☐ 23rd INF.
RGT.

☐ 5th BN., 23rd INFANTRY REGIMENT

☐ 25th DIVISION
'RAIDERS'

☐ 26th INFANTRY
REGIMENT

☐ 27th INFANTRY
REGIMENT

☐ 28th INFANTRY
REGIMENT

☐ 29th INFANTRY
REGIMENT

☐ 31st INFANTRY
REGIMENT

□ 31st INFANTRY REGIMENT

□ 31st INF. RGT., 7th DIV.

□ 32nd INF. REGIMENT

□ 34th INFANTRY REGIMENT

□ 34th INFANTRY REGIMENT

□ 3rd BN., 34th INFANTRY RGT.

□ 34th INF. RGT., 24th DIV.

□ 35th INF. RGT.

□ 36th INFANTRY REGIMENT

□ 39th INFANTRY REGIMENT

□ 3rd BN., 47th INFANTRY RGT.

□ 4th BN., 47th INF. RGT.

□ 48th INF. RGT.

□ 48th INF. RGT.

□ 51st INF. REGIMENT

□ 52nd INFANTRY SECURITY

□ 52nd INF. RGT.

□ 54th INFANTRY REGIMENT

□ 60th INFANTRY REGIMENT

□ 3rd BN., 60th INFANTRY RGT.

□ 1st BN., 60th INFANTRY REGIMENT

□ 69th INFANTRY REGIMENT

□ 71st INFANTRY REGIMENT

□ 137th INFANTRY REGIMENT

□ 155th INFANTRY REGIMENT

□ 161st INF. RGT.

□ CO. 'B'., 1st BN.,179th INFANTRY REGIMENT

□ 180th INF. RGT.

□ 271st INF. RGT.

□ 317th INFANTRY REGIMENT

□ 318th INFANTRY REGIMENT

□ 319th INFANTRY RGT.

INFANTRY UNITS

☐ 327th INFANTRY RGT., 93rd DIV.

☐ 335th INFANTRY REGIMENT

☐ 371st INF. REGIMENT

☐ 409th INF. REGIMENT

☐ 442nd INFANTRY REGIMENT

☐ 518th INF. REGIMENT

ARTILLERY

☐ 1st DIVISION ARTILLERY

☐ 2nd FLD. ARTY. BN.

☐ 3rd FIELD ARTY BN.

☐ 3rd DIVISION ARTILLERY

☐ 5th ARTILLERY

☐ 5th FIELD ARTY BN.

☐ 6th ARTILLERY

☐ 7th DIV. ARTILLERY

☐ 7th ARTILLERY

☐ 7th FIELD ARTY BN.

☐ 8th FIELD ARTY BN.

☐ 8th FLD. ARTY. BATTALION.

☐ 9th ARTILLERY

☐ 10th ARTILLERY

☐ 13th FLD. ARTILLERY BN.

☐ 15th ARTILLERY

☐ 18th FIELD ARTILLERY BN.

☐ 1st BN., 18th ARTILLERY

☐ 6th BN., 20th ARTILLERY

☐ 24th DIVISION ARTILLERY

☐ 28th FIELD ARTILLERY BN., 8th INFANTRY DIV.

113482

- [ ] 30th AAA BATTALION
- [ ] 32nd ARTY.
- [ ] 6th BN., 32nd ARTILLERY
- [ ] 33rd ARTILLERY
- [ ] 40th AAA BRIGADE
- [ ] 48th AAA BATTALION

- [ ] 52nd ARTILLERY BN.
- [ ] 64th FIELD ARTY. BN.
- [ ] 63rd FIELD ARTY. BN.
- [ ] 81st FIELD ARTY. BN.
- [ ] SEPARATE ARTILLERY BRIGADE

- [ ] 1st BN.,86th ARTY.
- [ ] 88th AAA BATTALION
- [ ] 90th ARTY. BN.
- [ ] 92nd ARTY. BATTALION
- [ ] 98th FIELD ARTILLERY BN.

- [ ] 114th ARTY.
- [ ] 159th ARTY. BN.
- [ ] 249th ARTY.
- [ ] 278th ARTY.
- [ ] 314th FIELD ARTY. BN.

- [ ] 141st FIELD ARTILLERY BN.

- [ ] 376th A/B ARTY. BN.
- [ ] 373rd FIELD ARTILLERY BN.
- [ ] 544th FIELD ARTILLERY BN.
- [ ] 524th FIELD ARTILLERY BN.
- [ ] 675th FIELD ARTILLERY BN.

| ☐ 1st INF. BRIGADE | ☐ 2nd INF. BRIGADE | ☐ 2nd A/B INF. BRIGADE | ☐ 11th INF. BRIGADE | ☐ 29th INF. BRIGADE (OLD) | ☐ 29th INF. BRIGADE | ☐ 36th INF. BRIGADE |

| ☐ 39th INF. BRIGADE | ☐ 41st INF. BRIGADE | ☐ 48th INF. BRIGADE | ☐ 49th INF. BRIGADE | ☐ 58th INF. BRIGADE | ☐ 67th INF. BRIGADE | ☐ 69th INF. BRIGADE |

| ☐ 72nd INF. BRIGADE | ☐ 73rd INF. BRIGADE | ☐ 75th INF. BRIGADE | ☐ 81st INF. BRIGADE | ☐ 91st INF. BRIGADE | ☐ 92nd INF. BRIGADE | ☐ 116th INF. BRIGADE |

  TAB ☐  TAB ☐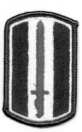

| ☐ 157th INF. BRIGADE | ☐ 171st INF. BRIGADE | ☐ 172nd INF. BRIGADE | ☐ 173rd A/B INF. BRIGADE | ☐ 187th INF. BRIGADE | ☐ 191st INF. BRIGADE | ☐ 193rd INF. BRIGADE |

| ☐ 196th INF. BRIGADE | ☐ 197th INF. BRIGADE | ☐ 198th INF. BRIGADE | ☐ 199th INF. BRIGADE | ☐ 205th INF. BRIGADE | ☐ 218th INF. BRIGADE | ☐ 256th INF. BRIGADE |

☐ 258th INF.
BRIGADE

☐ 278th INF.
BRIGADE

ARMORED BRIGADES

☐ 30th ARMD
BRIGADE

☐ 40th ARMD
BRIGADE

☐ 49th ARMD
BRIGADE

☐ 53rd ARMD
BRIGADE

☐ 86th ARMD
BRIGADE

☐ 149th ARMD
BRIGADE

☐ 155th ARMD
BRIGADE

☐ 194th ARMD
BRIGADE

ARTILLERY BRIGADES

☐ 11th AIR DEF.
ARTY BDE.

☐ 11th AIR DEF.
ARTILLERY

☐ 17th FIELD
ARTY BDE.

☐ 18th FIELD
ARTY BDE.

☐ 30th ARTY
BRIGADE

☐ 31st AIR DEF.
ARTY BDE.

☐ 32nd ARTY
BRIGADE

☐ 38th ARTY
BRIGADE

☐ 41st FIELD
ARTY BDE.

☐ 42nd FIELD
ARTY BDE.

☐ 56th ARTY
BRIGADE

☐ 57th FIELD
ARTY BDE.

☐ 72nd FIELD
ARTY BDE.

☐ 75th FIELD
ARTY BDE.

☐ 107th ARTY
BRIGADE

☐ 111th ARTY
BRIGADE

☐ 113th FIELD
ARTY BDE.

☐ 115th FIELD
ARTY BDE.
(1st DESIGN)

☐ 115th FLD.ARTY
BDE.(CURRENT)

☐ 118th FLD.
ARTY BDE.

☐ 130th FIELD
ARTY BDE.

BRIGADES

 ☐ 135th FIELD ARTY BDE.

 ☐ 138th FIELD ARTY BDE.

 ☐ 142nd FIELD ARTY BDE.

 ☐ 147th FIELD ARTY BDE.

 ☐ 151st FIELD ARTY BDE.

 ☐ 153rd FIELD ARTY BDE.

 ☐ 164th AIR DEF. ARTY BDE.

 ☐ 169th FIELD ARTY BDE.

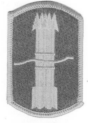 ☐ 196th FIELD ARTY BDE.

 ☐ 197th FIELD ARTY BDE.

 ☐ 209th FIELD ARTY BDE.

 ☐ 210th FIELD ARTY BDE.

 ☐ 212th FIELD ARTY BDE.

 ☐ 214th FIELD ARTY BDE.

 ☐ 227th FIELD ARTY BDE.

 ☐ 263rd AIR DEF. ARTY BDE.

 ☐ 313th FIELD ARTILLERY BN.

 ☐ 428th FIELD ARTY BDE.

TABS
1 - ☐
2 - ☐
3 - ☐
4 - ☐

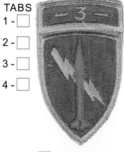 ☐ 3rd MISSILE COMMAND

 ☐ 479th FIELD ARTY BDE.

 ☐ 631st FIELD ARTY BDE.

 ☐ ANTI - AIRCRAFT COMMAND

 ☐ AIR DEFENSE COMMAND

ORDNANCE - MAINTENANCE

 ☐ 52nd ORDNANCE GROUP

 ☐ 57th ORDNANCE BRIGADE

 ☐ 59th ORDNANCE BRIGADE

 ☐ 701st MAINT. BATTALION

 ☐ BALLISTIC MISSILE AGENCY

 ☐ 711th MAINT. BATTALION

 ☐ 731st MAINT. BATTALION

 ☐ 794th MAINT. BATTALION

RANGERS

1ST ARMY RANGER CO.

2ND ARMY RANGER CO.

3RD ARMY RANGER CO.

4TH ARMY RANGER CO.

5TH ARMY RANGER CO.

6TH ARMY RANGER CO.

7TH ARMY RANGER CO.

8TH ARMY RANGER CO.

9TH ARMY RANGER CO.

10TH ARMY RANGER CO.

☐ HHC - 2/75th RANGERS

☐ "A" COMPANY 2/75th RANGERS

☐ "B" CO. 2/75th RANGERS

11TH ARMY RANGER CO.

12TH ARMY RANGER CO.

13TH ARMY RANGER CO.

14TH ARMY RANGER CO.

15TH ARMY RANGER CO.

75 RANGER RGT

☐ 7th RANGER BN.

RANGER

29TH RANGERS

18 RANGER INF.

1ST AIRBORNE RANGER CO.

2ND AIRBORNE RANGER CO.

3RD AIRBORNE RANGER CO.

4TH AIRBORNE RANGER CO.

5TH AIRBORNE RANGER CO.

8TH AIRBORNE RANGER CO.

AP RANGER CO.

DESERT RANGERS

1ST BN RANGER AIRBORNE 75TH INF.

□ SPECIAL FORCES

□ 10th SPECIAL FORCES GRP.

□ ARMY ELEMENTS SON TAY RAID

□ MIKE FORCE VIETNAM

□ MAC - V - SOG, MILITARY ASSISTANCE CMD., VIET NAM, STUDY OBSERVATION GROUP

□ JOINT SPECIAL OPERATIONS CMD.

□ U.S. SPECIAL OPERATIONS COMMAND, 1st DESIGN

□ U.S. SPECIAL OPERATIONS COMMAND, 2nd DESIGN

□ 1st SPECIAL OPERATIONS

□ SPECIAL MISSION ADVISORY GROUP

□ 5th SPECIAL FORCES GRP.

□ 10th SPECIAL FORCES

□ 46th SPECIAL FORCES

□ SPECIAL FORCES 'ODA - 5' (OPERATIONAL DETACHMENT-5)

□ SPECIAL FORCES 'ODA -6' (OPERATIONAL DETACHMENT-6)

□ A/B MIKE FORCE

□ SPECIAL OPERATIONS COMMAND

□ SPECIAL FORCES AVIATION

□ MOBILE TRAINING TEAM - 8A SPECIAL FORCES 'ODA -032' (OPERATIONAL DETACHMENT-032)

RECONDO

□ 9th RECONDO DIV.

□ 25th RECONDO DIV.

□ 25th RECONDO DIV.

□ 82nd A/B RECONDO DIV.

□ 101st A/B RECONDO DIV.

□ MAC - V RECONDO

☐ U.S. ARMY
AIR FORCE

☐ 1st AIR FORCE

☐ 2nd AIR FORCE

☐ 3rd AIR FORCE

☐ 4th AIR FORCE

☐ 5th AIR FORCE

☐ 6th AIR FORCE

☐ 7th AIR FORCE

☐ 8th AIR FORCE

☐ 9th AIR FORCE

☐ 10th AIR FORCE

☐ 11th AIR FORCE

☐ 12th AIR FORCE

☐ 13th AIR FORCE

☐ 14th AIR FORCE

☐ 15th AIR FORCE

☐ 18th AIR FORCE

☐ 20th AIR FORCE

☐ U.S. STRATEGIC
AIR FORCE

☐ U.S. ARMY AIRWAYS
COMMUNICATION SYS.

☐ DESERT AIR FORCE

☐ TROOP CARRIER
COMMAND

☐ U.S. AIR FORCE
EUROPE

☐ CUBAN AIR FORCE

☐ WOMEN'S AIR
FERRYING CMD.

☐ MILITARY AIR
TRANSPORT
SERVICE

☐ ALASKAN AIR
COMMAND

☐ CONTINENTAL
AIR COMMAND

☐ ALLIED AIR FORCE
MEDITERRANEAN

☐ AIR UNIVERSITY

☐ AIR MATERIAL
COMMAND

☐ U.S. ARMY AIR FORCE
HEADQUARTERS CMD.

☐ AIR TRANS.
COMMAND

☐ A/B TROOP
CARRIER

☐ AIR FERRYING
COMMAND

☐ AIR TRANS. CMD.
GROUND PERS.

☐ AIR TRAINING
COMMAND

☐ AIR FORCE
R.O.T.C.

☐ 9th ENGR.
COMMAND

☐ 12th TACTICAL
AIR FORCE

☐ PHILIPPINE
AIR FORCE

☐ FAR EAST AIR FORCE

☐ AIR TECHNICAL
SERVICE CMD.,
EUROPE

☐ COMBAT AIR CREW

☐ U.S. TECHNICAL
REPRESENTATIVE

☐ AIR FORCE CADET

☐ U.S. AIR FORCE
INSTRUCTOR

☐ U.S. AIR CORPS
(OLD)

☐ ARMY AIR FORCE
FLIGHT GUNNERY
SCHOOL

☐ WOMEN'S ARMY
SERVICE PILOT

☐ PHILIPPINE
AIR FORCE

☐ ARMY AF, HQ,
VARIATION

☐ THUNDERBIRD
FIELD, ARIZONA

☐ U.S. AAF FLIGHT
INSTRUCTOR

☐ AIR DEFENSE
COMMAND

☐ AIR FORCE
ENGINEERING
SPECIALIST

☐ AIR FORCE
PHOTOGRAPHY
SPECIALIST

☐ AIR FORCE
WEATHER
SPECIALIST

☐ AIR FORCE
ARMAMENT
SPECIALIST

☐ AIR FORCE
COMMUNICATION
SPECIALIST

☐ ALASKAN
AIR DEPOT

AAF ARCS

☐

☐

☐

☐

☐

☐

☐

AAF ARCS

☐ ALASKA AIR COMMAND

☐ INSTRUCTOR

☐ AIR UNIVERSITY

☐ AIR MATERIEL COMMAND

☐ AIR DEFENSE COMMAND

☐ TRAINING COMMAND

☐ PROVING GROUND COMMAND

☐ STRATEGIC AIR COMMAND

☐ A.A.F. WEATHER SERVICE

☐ AIR TECHNICAL SERVICE COMMAND

ARMY AVIATION

☐ I CORPS, AVIATION SECTION

☐ III CORPS, AVIATION SECTION

☐ 1st BDE.,1st CAV. DIV.

☐ 1st AVIATION BRIGADE

☐ 1st INFANTRY DIV. AVIATION CO.

☐ 1st INFANTRY DIV., AVIATION SECTION

☐ 1st ARMORED DIV. AVIATION CO.

☐ 1st CAV REGT. AVIATION

☐ "D" TROOP, 1st DIV., 1st AVN. PLT.

☐ 1st AVIATION CO.

☐ 3rd AVIATION COMPANY

☐ 3rd AVIATION BN.

☐ 4th SQUADRON, 3rd ARMORED CAVALRY REGT.

☐ 4th SQUADRON, 3rd ARMORED CAVALRY REGT.

☐ 4th SQUADRON, 3rd ARMORED CAVALRY REGT.

☐ 4th SQUADRON, 3rd ARMORED CAVALRY REGT.

☐ "Q" TROOP,4th SQUADRON, 3rd ARMD. CAV. REGT.

☐ 5th AVIATION BN.

☐ "A" TRP., 7th SQDN. 1st CAVALRY

☐ "D" TROOP, 10th AVIATION CO.

☐ HHC 10th AVIATION BN.

☐ 11th AVIATION BRIGADE

☐ 11th AIR CAVALRY REGIMENT

☐ 12th AVIATION BRIGADE

☐ 13th AVIATION BATTALION

☐ 16th MIL. POLICE AVIATION SEC.

☐ 17th AVN. BRIGADE

☐ "C" TRP., 7/17th CAVALRY REGIMENT

☐ 18th AVIATION BRIGADE

☐ 18th AVIATION CO.

☐ 20th ENGR. BDE. AVN. SECTION

☐ 21st INF. DIV. AVIATION

☐ "B" CO.; 25th AVIATION BN.

☐ 31st AVIATION CO.

☐ 71st ASLT HEL. CO.

☐ 73rd AVIATION CO.

☐ 81st AVIATION SECTION

☐ CO. "C", 101 ASSAULT HELI. BN.

☐ 92nd AVIATION CO.

☐ 116th AVIATION COMPANY

☐ 117th AVIATION CO.

☐ 117th ASSAULT HELICOPTER CO.

☐ 120th AVIATION COMPANY

ARMY AVIATION

☐ 128th AVIATION CO.

☐ 128th AVIATION CO.

☐ 156th ARMY
SECURITY
AGENCY, AVN. CO.

☐ 161st AVIATION
CO.

☐ 162nd ASSAULT
HELICOPTER CO.

☐ 165th AVIATION
GRP.

☐ CO. "E", 165th
AVIATION BN.

☐ 2nd PLT., 167th ASLT.
HELICOPTER CO.

☐ 170th ASSAULT
HELICOPTER CO.

☐ 174th AVIATION CO.

☐ 175th AVIATION
MAINT. BN.

☐ 178th AVIATION CO.

☐ 179th AVIATION CO.

☐ 179th PLT. / 402nd
TRANSPORTATION CO.

☐ 180th AVIATION
CO.

☐ 189th ASSAULT
HELICOPTER CO.

☐ 189th AVIATION
BN.

☐ 197th ARMED
HELI. CO.

☐ 2nd PLATOON,
198th AVN. CO.

☐ 201st AVIATION
COMPANY

☐ 219th AVIATION
COMPANY

☐ 223rd AVIATION
BN.

☐ 227th AVIATION CO.

☐ 227th ASSAULT
HELICOPTER BN.

☐ 229th AVIATION
BN.

PAGE 46

☐ 230th ASSAULT
HELICOPTER CO.

☐ 236th AVIATION CO.

☐ 269th COMBAT
AVIATION BN.

☐ 282nd ASLT.
HELI. CO.

☐ 335th ASSAULT
HELICOPTER CO.

☐ 362nd AVIATION
DETACHMENT

☐ 382nd AVIATION CO.

☐ 451st ASLT. HELI.
CO., AVIONICS
SECTION

☐ 478th AVIATION CO.
HEAVY HELICOPTER

☐ 484th TRANS. CO.
MAINT. DET.

☐ CO. "A" 501st
AVIATION BN.

☐ AH-64A APACHE
HELICOPTER

☐ NATIONAL TRAINING
CENTER OPFOR
AVIATION SECTION

☐ NATIONAL TRAINING
CENTER, FLIGHT DET.

☐ HELICOPTER SCH.
FLIGHT INSTR.

☐ FLIGHT OPERATIONS
DEFENSE LOGISTICS
AGENCY

☐ EXECUTIVE FLIGHT
DETACHMENT

☐ FORT LEAVENWORTH,
KANSAS AVIATION DIV.

☐ ARMY STUDENT PILOT

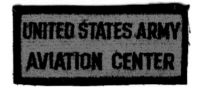

☐ ARMY AVIATION CENTER

☐ ARIZONA ARMY
AVIATION

☐ HELICOPTER SCHOOL ☐

☐ CH-47 "CHINOOK"

ARMY AVIATION

☐ COBRA GUNSHIPS ☐ COBRA GUNSHIPS ☐ COBRA GUNSHIPS ☐ GRUMMAN OV-1/RV-1 ARMY RECON AIRCRAFT

SCOUT DOGS

☐ 41st SCOUT DOG PLATOON ☐ 42nd SCOUT DOG PLATOON ☐ 49th INFANTRY SCOUT DOG PLT.

☐ 1st DOG PLATOON ☐ 2nd DIVISION, ARMY DOG HANDLER ☐ 34th - IPSD, INFANTRY POINT SCOUT DOG, 1st CAVALRY DIV. ☐ 48th SCOUT DOG, USMC ☐ K - 9 CORPS

☐ 62nd INFANTRY REGT. 'COMBAT TRACKERS' ☐ USMC "WAR DOGS" SENTRY DOGS ☐ 173rd A/B REGT., 39th SCOUT DOG PLATOON ☐ K - 9 CORPS

DISTINGUISHED UNIT CITATIONS

☐ 1st AWARD ☐ 2nd AWARD ☐ 3rd AWARD ☐ 4th AWARD ☐ 5th AWARD ☐ POST 1947 AIR FORCE

SIGNAL CORPS

☐ SIGNAL CORPS ☐ 1st SIGNAL BRIGADE ☐ 1st SIGNAL COMMAND ☐ 2nd SIGNAL BDE. ☐ 3rd SIGNAL BRIGADE ☐ 7th SIGNAL BRIGADE

☐ 7th RADIO RESEARCH UNIT

☐ 8th ARMY SIGNAL SCH.

☐ 11th SIGNAL BDE.

☐ 22nd SIGNAL BDE.

☐ 35th SIGNAL BDE.

☐ 39th SIGNAL BDE.

☐ 40th SIGNAL BATTALION

☐ 50th A/B SIGNAL BATTALION

☐ 77th SIGNAL BATTALION

☐ 93rd SIGNAL BDE.

☐ 121st SIGNAL BATTALION

☐ 123rd SIGNAL BN.

☐ 142nd SIGNAL BRIGADE

☐ 160th SIGNAL BDE.

☐ 187th SIGNAL BATTALION

☐ 228th SIGNAL BDE.

☐ 261st SIGNAL BRIGADE

☐ 335th SIGNAL BATTALION

☐ 359th SIGNAL BATTALION

☐ 511th SIGNAL BATTALION

☐ 848th SIGNAL TRAINING BN.

☐ 1101st SIGNAL BATTALION

☐ 1104th SIGNAL BATTALION

☐ 1106th SIGNAL BATTALION

☐ 1107th SIGNAL BDE.

☐ 1108th SIGNAL BDE.

☐ 1109th SIGNAL BATTALION

MEDICAL

 MEDIC'S ARMBAND

 1st MEDICAL BATTALION

 2nd MEDICAL BATTALION

 2nd MEDICAL BN

 2nd GENERAL MEDICAL DISP.

 3rd MEDICAL DET.

 3rd MEDICAL BATTALION

 4th MEDICAL BRIGADE

 7th MEDICAL BRIGADE

 7th MEDICAL COMMAND

 8th MEDICAL BRIGADE

 9th MEDICAL BN.

 18th MEDICAL BRIGADE

 34th MEDICAL BATTALION

 36th MEDICAL DET.

 36th MEDICAL DET.

 44th MEDICAL BRIGADE

 77th MEDICAL DET.

 93rd EVAC HOSPITAL

 100th MEDICAL BN

 102nd MEDICAL BATTALION

 106th MEDICAL BATTALION

 112th MEDICAL BRIGADE

 175th MEDICAL BRIGADE

 213th MEDICAL BRIGADE

 218th MEDICAL DET.

 229th MEDICAL DETACHMENT

PAGE 50

☐ 247th MEDICAL DET.

☐ 332nd MEDICAL BRIGADE

☐ 326th MEDICAL BATTALION

☐ 345th GENERAL MEDICAL DISP.

☐ 755th MEDICAL DET.

☐ 807th MED. BRIGADE

☐ 818th HOSPITAL CENTER

☐ MED. RESEARCH & DEVELOPMENT CMD.

☐ HEALTH & SERVICES COMMAND

☐ U.S. JOINT MIL. MED. CMD.

☐ MEDICAL COMMAND, EUROPE

☐ MEDICAL COMMAND, KOREA

☐ ARMY CRASH RESCUE

☐ AMERICAN RED CROSS MIL. WELFARE SRV.

☐ OCCUPATIONAL THERAPY

☐ OCCUPATIONAL THERAPY, APPRENTICE

☐ CADET NURSE

☐ 1st DIVISION MIL. POLICE

☐ 14th MIL. POLICE BDE.

☐ 15th MIL. POLICE BDE.

☐ 16th MILITARY POLICE BDE.

☐ 18th MIL. POLICE BDE.

☐ 43rd MILITARY POLICE BRIGADE

☐ 61st M.P. CO.

☐ 89th MILITARY POLICE BDE.

☐ 95th M.P. CO.

☐ 158th M.P. BATTALION

☐ 177th MILITARY POLICE BN.

MILITARY POLICE

☐ 220th MIL. POLICE BDE.

☐ 221st MIL. POLICE BDE.

☐ 260th MIL. POLICE BDE.

☐ 290th MIL. POLICE BDE.

☐ 300th MIL. POLICE BDE.

☐ 363rd M.P. CO.

ENGINEERS

☐ 1st ENGINEER BATTALION

☐ 3rd ENGINEER BN.

☐ 3rd ENGR.

☐ 7th ENGINEER BRIGADE

☐ 16th ENGR. BDE.

☐ 18th ENGINEER BRIGADE

☐ 20th ENGINEER BRIGADE

☐ 30th ENGR. BRIGADE

☐ 36th ENGR. BATTALION

☐ 37th ENGINEER BATTALION

☐ 82nd ENGINEER BATTALION

☐ 127th ENGR. BATTALION

☐ 130th ENGR. BRIGADE

☐ 168th ENGR. BATTALION

☐ 169th ENGR. BATTALION

☐ 194th ENGR. BRIGADE

☐ 411th ENGR. BRIGADE

☐ 411th ENGR. BRIGADE

☐ 412th ENGR. BRIGADE

☐ 416th ENGR. BRIGADE

☐ 420th ENGR. BRIGADE

☐ 510/213th ENGINEER DETACHMENT

☐ 839th ENGINEER AVIATION GROUP

☐ 891st ENGINEER BATTALION

☐ 1778th ENGINEER BATTALION

☐ CORPS OF ENGINEERS LOCK & DAM TENDER

☐ ENGINEER CMD. EUROPE

ENGINEER CMD. VIETNAM

 TAB ☐

 TAB ☐

TAB ☐

☐ ENGINEER SPECIAL BRIGADES

☐ ENGINEER TECHNICAL INTELLIGENCE TEAM

☐ CORPS OF ENGINEERS

☐ ARMY MAP SERVICE

CIVIL AFFAIRS BRIGADES

☐ 351st CIVIL AFFAIRS BDE.

☐ 352nd CIVIL AFFAIRS BDE.

☐ 353rd CIVIL AFFAIRS BDE.

☐ 354th CIVIL AFFAIRS BDE.

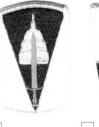

☐ 356th CIVIL AFFAIRS BDE.

☐ 357th CIVIL AFFAIRS BDE.

☐ 358th CIVIL AFFAIRS BDE.

☐ 360th CIVIL AFFAIRS BDE.

☐ 361st CIVIL AFFAIRS BDE.

☐ 362nd CIVIL AFFAIRS BDE.

☐ 363rd CIVIL AFFAIRS BDE.

☐ 364th CIVIL AFFAIRS BDE.

☐ 365th CIVIL AFFAIRS BDE.

MILITARY INTELLIGENCE

☐ HHC; 1st MILITARY INTELLIGENCE BN.

☐ 2nd MILITARY INTEL. CMD.

☐ 66th MILITARY INTEL. BDE.

☐ 201st MILITARY INTEL. CMD.

☐ 205th MILITARY INTELLIGENCE BDE.

MILITARY INTELLIGENCE

☐ 207th MILITARY INTEL. BDE.
☐ 300th MIL. INTEL. BDE.
☐ 319th MIL. INTEL. BDE.
☐ 470th MIL. INTEL. BDE.
☐ 500th MIL. INTEL. BDE.
☐ 501st MIL. INTEL. BDE.
☐ 504th MIL. INTEL. BDE.

☐ 513th MILITARY INTELLIGENCE BDE.
☐ 525th MILITARY INTELLIGENCE BDE.
☐ U.S. INTELLIGENCE COMMAND
☐ U.S. INTELLIGENCE AGENCY
☐ INTELLIGENCE & SECURITY CMD.

☐ 332nd ARMY SECURITY AGENCY
☐ MILITARY INTEL. OCCUPIED JAPAN
☐ ARMY SECURITY EXCHANGE
☐ ARMY SECURITY AGENCY
☐ INTELLIGENCE AGENCY

TRANSPORTATION CORPS

☐ PORTS OF EMBARKATION
☐ TRANSPORTATION COMMAND
☐ 1st SUPPLY & TRANS. BN.
☐ 2nd TRANS. BRIGADE
☐ 3rd TRANS. BRIGADE

☐ 4th TRANS. BRIGADE
☐ 5th TRANS. BRIGADE
☐ 7th TRANS. BRIGADE
☐ 9th TRANS. BN.

☐ 11th TRANS. BN.
☐ 24th TRANSPORTATION & SUPPLY BATTALION
☐ 27th TRANS. BN.
☐ 32nd TRANS.BDE.

☐ 35th TRANS. BATTALION

☐ 40th TRANSPORTATION SUPPLY & SUPPORT CO.

☐ 107th TRANS. BRIGADE

☐ 124th TRANS. BRIGADE

☐ 125th TRANS. BRIGADE

☐ 143rd TRANS. BRIGADE

TAB
☐

☐ 167th TRANS. DETACHMENT

☐ 184th TRANS. BRIGADE

☐ 319th TRANS. BRIGADE

☐ PATCH

☐ 425th TRANS. BRIGADE

☐ 425th TRANSPORTATION SUPPLY & SUPPORT BN.

☐

☐

☐

☐

☐

☐

TRANSPORTATION TERMINAL CMDS.

SUPPORT UNITS

☐ 1st SUPPORT BRIGADE

☐ 2nd SUPPORT BRIGADE

☐ 3rd SUPPORT BRIGADE

☐ 7th ARMY SUPPORT COMMAND

☐ 8th ARMY FIELD SUPPORT COMMAND

☐ 12th SUPPORT BRIGADE

☐ 13th SUPPORT BRIGADE

☐ 15th SUPPORT BRIGADE

☐ 19th SUPPORT BRIGADE

☐ 22nd SUPPORT BRIGADE

SUPPORT UNITS

 ☐ 23rd SUPPORT BRIGADE

 ☐ 169th SUPPORT BN.

 ☐ 167th SUPPORT BRIGADE

 ☐ 377th SUPPORT BRIGADE

 ☐ ADVANCED WEAPONS SUPPORT COMMAND

 ☐ ALASKAN SUPPORT COMMAND

 ☐ DEFENSE ATOMIC SUPPORT CMD.

 ☐ DEFENSE ATOMIC SUPPORT CMD.

 ☐ SPECIAL AMMUNITION SUPPORT CMD.

 ☐ U.S.A. SUPPORT THAILAND CMD.

ARMY RESERVE COMMANDS

 ☐ 7th ARCOM

 ☐ 120th ARCOM

 ☐ 121st ARCOM

 ☐ 122nd ARCOM

 ☐ 123rd ARCOM

 ☐ 124th ARCOM

☐ 125th ARCOM

NATIONAL GUARD HEADQUARTERS

 ☐ ALABAMA

 ☐ ALASKA

 ☐ ARIZONA (OLD)

 ☐ ARIZONA (CURRENT)

 ☐ ARKANSAS

 ☐ CALIFORNIA

 ☐ COLORADO

 ☐ CONNECTICUT (OLD)

 ☐ CONNECTICUT

☐ DELAWARE ☐ FLORIDA ☐ GEORGIA ☐ GUAM ☐ HAWAII ☐ IDAHO (OLD)

☐ IDAHO ☐ ILLINOIS ☐ INDIANA ☐ IOWA (OLD) ☐ IOWA ☐ KANSAS

☐ KENTUCKY ☐ KENTUCKY, INSTRUCTOR ☐ LOUISIANA ☐ MAINE ☐ MARYLAND ☐ MASSACHUSETTS

☐ MICHIGAN ☐ MINNESOTA ☐ MISSISSIPPI ☐ MISSOURI ☐ MONTANA ☐ NEBRASKA

☐ NEVADA ☐ NEW HAMPSHIRE ☐ NEW JERSEY ☐ NEW MEXICO (OLD) ☐ NEW MEXICO ☐ NEW YORK (OLD)

☐ NEW YORK ☐ NORTH CAROLINA ☐ NORTH DAKOTA ☐ OHIO ☐ OKLAHOMA ☐ OREGON

NATIONAL GUARD HEADQUARTERS

☐ PENNSYLVANIA ☐ RHODE ISLAND ☐ SOUTH CAROLINA ☐ SOUTH DAKOTA ☐ TENNESSEE ☐ TEXAS

☐ UTAH (OLD) ☐ UTAH ☐ VERMONT (OLD) ☐ VERMONT ☐ VIRGINIA ☐ WASHINGTON

☐ WEST VIRGINIA ☐ WISCONSIN ☐ WYOMING ☐ PUERTO RICO ☐ VIRGIN ISLANDS ☐ WASHINGTON D.C.

LOGISTICAL COMMANDS (U.S. ARMY)

☐ 1st LOG. CMD. ☐ 2nd LOG. CMD. (OLD) ☐ 2nd LOG. CMD. ☐ 3rd LOG. CMD. ☐ 4th LOG. CMD. ☐ 5th LOG. CMD. ☐ 7th LOG. CMD.

☐ 8th LOG. CMD. ☐ 9th LOG. CMD. ☐ 300th LOG. CMD. ☐ 301st LOG. CMD. ☐ 304th LOG. CMD. ☐ 305th LOG. CMD. ☐ 307th LOG. CMD.

☐ 310th LOG. CMD. ☐ 311th LOG. CMD. ☐ 312th LOG. CMD. ☐ 313th LOG. CMD. ☐ 315th LOG. CMD. ☐ 316th LOG. CMD. ☐ 318th LOG. CMD.

LOGISTICAL COMMANDS

 ☐ 319th LOG. CMD.

 ☐ 320th LOG. CMD.

 ☐ 321st LOG. CMD.

 ☐ 322nd LOG. CMD.

 ☐ 323rd LOG. CMD.

 ☐ 324th LOG. CMD.

 ☐ 325th LOG. CMD.

 ☐ 505th GRAVE REGISTRATION UNIT, 1st LOGISTICAL CMD.

 ☐ LABOR SERVICE

 ☐ EUROPEAN LABOR SERVICE

 ☐ GERMAN LABOR SERVICE

 ☐ ARMY LOGISTIC CENTER

 ☐ JAPANESE LOG. CMD.

 ☐ QUARTERMASTER

SCHOOLS - CENTERS - ACADEMIES

 ☐ ADMINISTRATION CENTER & SCHOOL

 ☐ AIR DEFENSE SCHOOL

 ☐ ARTILLERY & MISSILE SCH.

 ☐ ARMED FORCES INFORMATION SCH.

 ☐ AIRBORNE SCHOOL

 ☐ ARMY WAR COLLEGE

 ☐ AVIATION ENGINEER SCHOOL

 ☐ AVIATION SCHOOL

 ☐ INFANTRY SCHOOL

 ☐ CIVIL AFFAIRS SCHOOL

 ☐ FIXED WING AVIATION SCHOOL

 ☐ CMD. & GENERAL STAFF SCHOOL

 ☐ COMBAT SURVEILLANCE ELECTRONIC WARFARE SCHOOL

 ☐ DRILL INSTRUCTOR SCHOOL

 ☐ FIELD ARTILLERY SCHOOL ☐

SCHOOLS - CENTERS - ACADEMIES

☐ OFFICER CANDIDATE SCHOOL

☐ SCHOOL OF THE AMERICAS

☐ ADJUTANT GENERAL CENTER & SCHOOL

☐ HELICOPTER SCHOOL

TAB
☐

☐ JUNGLE SCHOOL

☐ UNIVERSITY OF HEALTH SCIENCES, UNIFORMED SERVICES

☐ JUDGE ADVOCATE GENERAL SCHOOL

☐ SPECIAL WARFARE SCHOOL

☐ SERGEANT MAJOR ACADEMY

☐ WEST POINT CADET

☐ WEST POINT ASSIGNED PERSONNEL

☐ WEST POINT CADET

☐ RANGER DEPARTMENT INFANTRY SCHOOL

☐ A/B SCHOOL, MAINZ, GERMANY

☐ COMBAT LEADERSHIP TRAINEE

☐ 402nd TRAINING BRIGADE

☐ 5th TRAINING BDE.

☐ JUNGLE SCHOOL

☐ U.S. ARMY FOOD SERVICE SCHOOL

☐ QM. CENTER & SCH.

☐ QM. CENTER & SCH.

☐ MILITARY INTEL. CENTER & SCH.

☐ SIGNAL CORPS CENTER & SCH.

☐ ENGINEER CTR. & SCH.

☐ MISSILE & MUNITIONS CTR. & SCH.

☐ CHEM. CORPS CTR. & SCH.

☐ MEDICAL CTR. & SCH.

☐ MIL. POLICE CTR. & SCH.

☐ ORDNANCE CTR. & SCH.

☐ TRANSPORTATION SCHOOL

☐ NATIONAL TRAINING CENTER

☐ 2nd TRAINING REGT.

☐ UNIVERSAL MILITARY TRAINING, (SHOULDER)

☐ UNIVERSAL MILITARY TRAINING, (CAP)

☐ U.S. ARMY SHOOTING TEAM

☐ NATIONAL SECURITY TRAINING

MILITARY AID & ADVISOR UNITS

☐ AGGRESSOR FORCE

☐ USMAC THAILAND

☐ U.S. MAAG CAMBODIA

☐ MAAG FORMOSA

☐ MAAG LAOS INSTRUCTOR

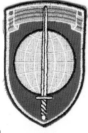

☐ MAAG LAOS

☐ MAAG LAOS

☐ MAAG THAILAND

☐ MAAG VIET NAM

☐ MAAG INDONESIA

☐ FREE WORLD MIL. FORCES, VN.

☐ USA VIET NAM

☐ 1st FIELD FORCE, VN

☐ 2nd FIELD FORCE, VN

☐ MIL. ASSISTANCE CMD., VIET NAM

☐ SECURITY FORCE VIET NAM

☐ SUPREME HQ ALLIED POWERS, EUROPE

☐ H.Q. ALLIED FORCES SOUTHEAST EUROPE

☐ H.Q. ALLIED FORCES SOUTHERN EUROPE

☐ KAGNEW STATION ASMARA, ERITRIA

☐ 2506th SPECIAL BRIGADE "BAY OF PIGS"

☐ U.S. SOUTHERN EUROPE TASK FORCE

☐ ALLIED LAND FORCES, CENTRAL EUROPE

AID & ADVISOR

☐ KOREAN CIVIL
ASSISTANCE
COMMAND

☐ TAB

☐ U.S. FORCES DOMINICAN
REPUBLIC

☐ MILITARY TRAINING MISSION
SAUDI ARABIA

☐ U.S.- TAIWAN DEFENSE
COMMAND

☐ H.Q. ALLIED FORCES
CENTRAL EUROPE,
STAFF

☐ H.Q. AFCE
ARMY

☐ H.Q. AFCE
AIR FORCE

☐ H.Q. AFCE
NAVY

☐ ALLIED MOBILE
FORCE, EUROPE

☐ MULTINATIONAL
FORCE
& OBSERVERS

☐ U.S. ARMY MISSION

☐ MULTINATIONAL FORCES, BERET

COMMANDS

☐ CAPITOL MILITARY
ASSISTANCE CMD.

☐ U.S. ARMY STRATEGIC
REACTION COMMAND

☐ 55th COMMAND
HEAD QUARTERS

☐ JOINT READINESS
COMMAND

☐ SELECTIVE
SERVICE

☐ ARMY SPACE
COMMAND

☐ ARMY MATERIAL
COMMAND

☐ COMBAT
DEVELOPMENTS
COMMAND

☐ CRIMINAL INVESTIGATION
DIVISION (C.I.D.)

☐ COMPUTER SYSTEMS
COMMAND

☐ STRATEGIC
COMMUNICATION CMD.

PAGE 62

☐ SENTINEL SYSTEMS
COMMAND

☐ U.S. FORCES
IN EUROPE

☐ INFORMATION & DATA
SYSTEMS COMMAND

☐ 156th QM.
COMMAND

☐ TEST & EXPERIMENTATION COMMAND

☐ INFORMATION SERVICES, ENGINEERING CMD.

☐ MILITARY ENTRANCE PROCESSING COMMAND ARMY ELEMENTS

☐ CENTRAL COMMAND

PERSONNEL RELATED

☐ 1st PERSONNEL COMMAND

☐ 3rd PERSONNEL COMMAND

☐ 8th PERSONNEL COMMAND

☐ 10th PERSONNEL COMMAND

☐ MILITARY PERSONNEL CENTER

☐ TOTAL ARMY PERSONNEL AGENCY

☐ INDIVIDUAL READINESS RESERVE

☐ ARMY BROADCAST SERVICE

☐ COMMUNITY & FAMILY SUPPORT CENTER

☐ 175th FINANCE CENTER

☐ U.S. ARMY BAND

☐ 266th FINANCE CENTER

☐ ARMY HOSTESS

☐ U.S.O. CAMP SHOWS

☐ ARMY LEGAL SERVICES

☐ WAR CORRESPONDENT

☐ WAR PHOTOGRAPHER

☐ ARMY PHOTOGRAPHER

☐ WAR CORRESPONDENT

☐ U.S.A. BAND

☐ STARS & STRIPES PACIFIC

☐ ARMED FORCES NETWORK, EUROPE

☐ U.S. & WACs HQ. CO.

☐ YANK CORRESPONDENT

☐ HARBOR NET TENDER

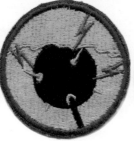

☐ MINECRAFT PERSONNEL

☐ PATROL TORPEDO BOATS

☐ PATROL TORPEDO BOATS

☐ U.S. MARITIME SCHOOL

☐ EX-NAVY

☐ CONSTRUCTION BN.

☐ CONSTRUCTION BN. "SEABEES"

☐ NAVAL AMPHIBIOUS FORCES

☐ NAVAL AMPHIBIOUS FORCES

☐ SUPERVISOR OF SALVAGE

☐ EXPERIMENTAL DIVING UNIT

☐ BASIC UNDER-WATER DIVING SCH. INSTRUCTOR

☐ BASIC UNDERWATER DIVING SCHOOL, SUPPORT STAFF

☐ NAV/SWG-VN

☐ NAV/SWG-1 STAFF

☐ SEAL TEAM-1

☐ SEAL TEAM-2

☐ SEAL TEAM-3

☐ SEAL TEAM-4

☐ SEAL TEAM-5

☐ SEAL TEAM-6

☐ SEAL SUPPORT TEAM 2

☐ UNDERWATER DEMOLITION TEAM 11

☐ UNDERWATER DEMOLITION TEAM 12

☐ UNDERWATER DEMOLITION TEAM 121

☐ SUBMERSIBLE DIVING VEHICLE TEAM 2

☐ SUBMERSIBLE DIVING VEHICLE TEAM 22

☐ RIVER ASSAULT FLOTILLA 1

☐ RIVER PATROL FORCE TF-116

☐ RIVER SQDN. 51

☐ RIVER DIV. 52

☐ RIVER DIV. 512

☐ RIVER DIV. 524

☐ RIVER DIV. 532

☐ RIVER DIV. 533

☐ RIVER DIV. 543

☐ RIVER DIV. 571

☐ RIVER DIV. 573

☐ RIVER DIV. 591

☐ INSHORE UNDERSEA WARFARE, GROUP-1

☐ USN PARA TEAM

☐ USN PARA TEAM

☐ INSHORE UNDERSEA WARFARE, GROUP-3, UNIT 2

☐ JUNGLE ENVIRONMENTAL SURVIVAL TRAINING

☐ MOBILE INSHORE UNDERSEA WARFARE, GROUP-2122

☐ MOBILE INSHORE UNDERSEA WARFARE, UNIT-12

☐ INSHORE UNDERSEA WARFARE, GROUP-1

PAGE 65

☐ 1st MARINE
DIVISION

☐ 2nd MARINE
DIVISION

☐ 2nd MARINE
DIVISION

☐ 3rd MARINE
DIVISION

☐ 4th MARINE
DIVISION

☐ 5th MARINE
DIVISION (OLD)

☐ 5th MARINE
DIVISION

☐ 6th MARINE
DIVISION

☐ 4th MARINE
BASE DEFENSE
AIR WING

☐ 13th MARINE
DEFENSE BN.

☐ 18th MARINE
DEFENSE BN.

☐ 51st DEFENSE BN.

☐ 52nd DEFENSE BN.

☐ MARINE SHIP
DETACHMENT
AFLOAT
'SEA MARINES'

☐ MARINE DET:
LONDONDERRY

☐ MARINE DETACHMENT
ICELAND

☐ PACIFIC AIR WING
HEADQUARTERS

☐ 1st MARINE AIR WING

☐ 2nd MARINE AIR WING

☐ 3rd MARINE AIR WING

☐ 4th MARINE AIR WING

☐ FMF HONOR GUARD

☐ FMF PACIFIC HQ.

☐ FMF PACIFIC
ENGINEER BN.

☐ FMF PACIFIC
SUPPLY

☐ FMF - PAC PACIFIC DUKW COMPANIES

☐ FMF PACIFIC ARTILLERY BN.

☐ FMF PACIFIC ANTI-AIRCRAFT ARTILLERY

☐ FMF PACIFIC TRACTOR BN.

☐ FMF PACIFIC BOMB DISPOSAL CO.

☐ FMF PACIFIC DOG PLATOON

☐ 1st M.A.C. HEAD-QUARTERS

☐ 1st M.A.C. ARTY.

☐ 1st M.A.C. AVIATION ENGINEERS

☐ 1st M.A.C. BARRAGE BALLOON BN.

☐ 1st M.A.C. DEFENSE BN.

☐ 1st M.A.C. PARATROOPS

☐ 1st M.A.C. RAIDERS

☐ 1st M.A.C. SERVICE SUPPLY BN.

☐ 3rd AMPHIBIOUS CORPS

☐ 5th AMPHIBIOUS CORPS

☐ 704th MARINE RAIDER BN.

☐ MARINE AIRCRAFT HEADQUARTERS PACIFIC WINGS

☐ AIRCRAFT FUSELAGE 1st WING

☐ AIRCRAFT FUSELAGE 2nd WING

☐ AIRCRAFT FUSELAGE 3rd WING

☐ AIRCRAFT FUSELAGE 4th WING

☐ USMC AIRBORNE VIET NAM

☐ 1st MARINE BRIGADE FLEET MARINE FORCE

☐ U.S.M.C. UNOFFICIAL

PAGE 67

MARINE CORPS

☐ 1st MARINE DIV. HQ. BN.

☐ 1st MARINES - 2nd BN. "THE PROFESSIONALS"

☐ 1st MARINE DIV. 3rd BN. "GUERRILLAS"

☐ 3rd MARINE DIV.

☐ 3rd MARINE DIVISION 1st DEFENSE BN.

☐ 3rd MARINE DIV. 3rd REGT.; 3rd BN.

☐ 3rd MARINE DIVISION SNIPER PLATOON

☐ 1st MARINE REGIMENT

☐ 2nd MARINE REGIMENT

☐ 3rd MARINE REGIMENT

☐ 4th MARINE REGT.

☐ 4th MARINES; 3rd BN. "THUNDERING THIRD"

☐ 1st BATTALION, 5th REGIMENT

☐ 2nd BATTALION, 5th REGIMENT

☐ 3rd BATTALION, 5th REGIMENT

☐ 7th MARINE REGIMENT

☐ 7th MARINES "SEBUN MARINES"

☐ 9th MARINES

☐ 9th MARINE REGIMENT

☐ 9th MARINE EXPEDITIONARY BRIGADE

☐ 2 BN.; 9th MARINE REGIMENT; "HELL IN A HELMET"

☐ 10th MARINE REGIMENT

☐ 11th MARINE REGIMENT

☐ 2nd BATTALION, 11th REGIMENT

☐ 5th BATTALION, 11th REGIMENT

☐ 12th MARINE REGIMENT

☐ 23rd MARINE REGIMENT

☐ 23rd MARINES; 2nd BN., WEAPONS COMPANY

☐ 24th MARINE REGIMENT

☐ 26th MARINE REGIMENT

☐ MARINE SHIP DETACHMENT CV-41 USS MIDWAY

☐ 1st RECON BN.

☐ 1st RECON CO.

☐ 1st MARINE DIV. (LRRP) LONG RANGE RECON PATROL

☐ 1st RECON BN. SNIPER PLATOON

☐ 1st TANK BN.

☐ 1st TANK BN.

☐ 1st LIGHT ARMORED INFANTRY BN.

☐ 1st RECON BN., LIGHT ARMORED

☐ 1st COMBAT ENGINEER BN.

☐ 1st AIR-NAVAL GUNFIRE LIAISON CO.

☐ 1st MARINE BRIGADE ICELAND

☐ 1st MARINE DIV. CHINA SERVICE GRP.

☐ 1st MARINE DIV. AAA GUN BN.

☐ 1st LANDING SUPPORT BATTALION

☐ 1st FORCE RECON CO. (FMF) - PACIFIC

☐ 1st DEFENSE BN. (FMF)

☐ 1st DEFENSE BN.

☐ 1st MARINE DIVISION SPECIAL SERVICE TROOP

MARINE CORPS

☐ 1st MARINES - 3rd BATTALION SPECIAL LANDING FORCE

☐ 1st MARINE DIVISION TRUCK COMPANY

☐ 1st FLEET MARINE FORCE-PACIFIC, SERVICE SUPPORT GROUP

☐ 1st MEDICAL BN., 1st FORCE SERVICE SUPPORT GROUP

☐ 1st MARINE DIVISION SCOUT- SNIPER SCHOOL

☐ 1st COMBAT ENGINEER BN.

☐ 1st RADIO COMPANY FLEET MARINE FORCE

☐ 2nd MARINE DIVISION 2nd RECON BN.

☐ 2nd MARINE DIVISION 2nd SCOUTS

☐ 2nd MARINE DIVISION 2nd FORCE RECON FMF - ATLANTIC

☐ 2nd MARINE DIVISION 2nd FORCE RECON FMF - ATLANTIC

☐ 2nd LIGHT ANTI-AIRCRAFT MISSILE BATTALION

☐ 3rd MARINE DIVISION RECON BN.

☐ 3rd MARINE DIVISION 3rd RECON BN.

☐ 3rd LIGHT ARMORED RECON BN.'WOLF PACK'

☐ 3rd AMPHIBIOUS TRUCK CO.

☐ 3rd ASSAULT AMPHIBIOUS BN.

☐ 3rd LOW-ALTITUDE AIR DEFENSE BN.

☐ 3rd LIGHT ARMORED INFANTRY BN.

☐ 4th LOW - ALTITUDE AIR DEFENSE BN.

☐ 5th COMBINED EXPEDITIONARY BRIGADE

☐ 5th M.A.C.; 16 AAA BN. (LIGHT)

☐ 5th M.A.C.; 16 AAA BN., (HEAVY)

☐ 7th ENGINEER BN.

☐ LIGHT ARMORED VEHICLE
TEST DIRECTORATE

☐ 15th MARINE EXPEDITIONARY UNIT
AIR-GROUND TASK FORCE

☐ MARINE EXPEDITIONARY FORCE
AIR-GROUND TEAM

☐ MARINE EXPEDITIONARY
FORCE, AIR-GROUND TEAM 2

☐ MARINE EXPEDITIONARY
FORCE, AIR-GROUND TEAM 3

☐ MARINE EXPEDITIONARY
FORCE, AIR-GROUND TEAM 5

☐ LANDING TASK FORCE
COMMAND PACIFIC

☐ BULLET STOPPER - TANK

☐ EXPLOSIVE ORDNANCE
DISPOSAL

☐ PENDLETON FIELD
MEDICAL SERVICE
SCHOOL

☐ AIR - GROUND COMBAT
CENTER, 29 PALMS

☐ U.S.M.C. SECURITY
FORCE - ADAK

☐ U.S.M.C. FORCE RECON

☐ MILITARY POLICE

☐ U.S.M.C. FORCE RECON
VIETNAM

☐ U.S.M.C. FORCE RECON

☐ U.S.M.C. FORCE RECON

MARINE CORPS

☐ U.S.M.C. PATHFINDER

☐ U.S.M.C. MASTER OF FITNESS

☐ U.S.M.C.FORCE LOG. COMMAND, VIETNAM

☐ ASSAULT AMPHIBIAN SCH. CAMP PENDLETON

☐ U.S.M.C. MAAG TAIWAN

☐ U.S.M.C. IN LEBANON

☐ COMMUNICATION & ELECTRONICS SCHOOL

☐ SCHOOL OF INFANTRY CAMP PENDLETON

☐ AIRBORNE MARINES

☐ U.S. MARINE ADVISORS ROYAL SAUDI MARINES

☐ HAZARDOUS MATERIALS TEAM, LIGHT ATTACK HELICOPTER, SQDN - 169

☐ MARINE OBSERVATION SQUADRON 2

☐ OPERATION JUST CAUSE, PANAMA

☐ TASK FORCE PAPA BEAR, DESERT STORM

☐ OPERATION DESERT STORM, PERSIAN GULF WAR

☐ OPERATION RESTORE HOPE, SOMALIA

☐ TAB

☐ U.S. FORCES PERSIAN GULF WAR

☐ U.S. FORCES PERSIAN GULF WAR

☐ TAB

☐ STORM TROOPER - TAB OPERATION DESERT STORM

☐ TAB

☐ TAB

☐ TAB

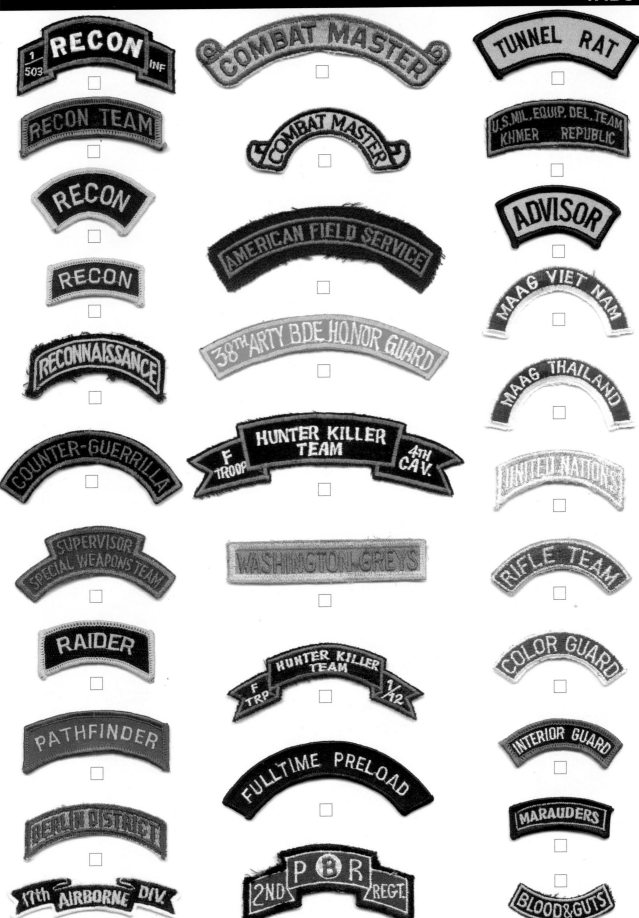

RECON 1 503 INF

RECON TEAM

RECON

RECON

RECONNAISSANCE

COUNTER-GUERRILLA

SUPERVISOR SPECIAL WEAPONS TEAM

RAIDER

PATHFINDER

BERLIN DISTRICT

17th AIRBORNE DIV.

COMBAT MASTER

COMBAT MASTER

AMERICAN FIELD SERVICE

38TH ARTY BDE HONOR GUARD

HUNTER KILLER TEAM F TROOP 4TH CAV.

WASHINGTON GREYS

HUNTER KILLER TEAM F TRP 1/A2

FULLTIME PRELOAD

2ND P B R REGT.

TUNNEL RAT

U.S. MIL. EQUIP. DEL. TEAM KHMER REPUBLIC

ADVISOR

MAAG VIET NAM

MAAG THAILAND

UNITED NATIONS

RIFLE TEAM

COLOR GUARD

INTERIOR GUARD

MARAUDERS

BLOOD & GUTS

TABS

CONSTABULARY ☐

LRRP ☐

LRRP ☐

LRRP ☐

LRRP ☐

LRRP ☐

LRRP ☐

LRRP ☐

SNIPER ☐

TANK 752 BN ☐

VIETNAM ☐

VIETNAM ☐

VIETNAM ☐

VIETNAM ☐

2PBN HAWK SECURITY GUARD 71ST ARTY ☐

COMMANDO ☐

GERMANY ☐

GERMANY ☐

USAFACFS SALUTE BTRY ☐

PUERTO RICO NATIONAL GUARD ☐

DRILL TEAM ☐

DRILL TEAM ☐

VIENNA ☐

BASE HONOR GUARD ☐

PERSHING RIFLES ☐

PERSHING RIFLES ☐

AIRBORNE ☐

AIRBORNE ☐

AIRBORNE ☐

AIRBORNE ☐

AIRBORNE ☐

AIRBORNE ☐

AIRBORNE ☐

AIRBORNE ☐

GRENADA ☐

GRENADA ☐

GRENADA ☐

GRENADA ☐

GRENADA ☐

GRENADA ☐

CIVIL AIR PATROL

☐ CIVIL AIR PATROL

☐ AUXILIARY AIR FORCE

☐ EMERGENCY SERVICES

☐ CIVIL AIR PATROL
USAAF H.Q.

☐ CADET

☐ ALABAMA

☐ ALASKA (OLD)

☐ ALASKA

☐ ARIZONA

☐ ARKANSAS

☐ CALIFORNIA

☐ COLORADO

☐ CONNECTICUT

☐ DELAWARE

☐ FLORIDA

☐ GEORGIA

☐ HAWAII

☐ IDAHO

☐ ILLINOIS

☐ INDIANA

☐ IOWA

☐ KANSAS

☐ KENTUCKY

☐ LOUISIANA

☐ MAINE ☐ MARYLAND ☐ MASSACHUSETTS ☐ MICHIGAN ☐ MINNESOTA

☐ MISSISSIPPI ☐ MISSOURI ☐ MONTANA ☐ NEBRASKA

☐ NEVADA ☐ NEW HAMPSHIRE ☐ NEW JERSEY ☐ NEW MEXICO ☐ NEW YORK

☐ NORTH CAROLINA ☐ NORTH DAKOTA ☐ OHIO ☐ OKLAHOMA ☐ OREGON (OLD)

☐ OREGON ☐ PENNYSLYVANIA ☐ PUERTO RICO ☐ RHODE ISLAND ☐ SOUTH CAROLINA

☐ SOUTH DAKOTA ☐ TENNESSEE (OLD) ☐ TENNESSEE ☐ TEXAS PAGE 77

CIVIL AIR PATROL

☐ UTAH

☐ VERMONT

☐ VIRGINIA

☐ WASHINGTON

☐ WEST VIRGINIA

☐ WISCONSIN

☐ WYOMING

☐ WASHINGTON D.C.

☐ LIAISON PATROL SOUTHERN

☐ SHOOTING PROFICIENCY

☐ C.A.P. ENCAMPMENT

☐ C.A.P. CAP PATCH

☐ CADET P.F.C.

☐ CADET CORPORAL

☐ CADET SGT.

☐ CADET FIRST SGT.

☐ MECHANICAL PROFICIENCY

☐ RADIO PROFICIENCY

☐ NAME STRIP

☐ HQ. STAFF CA. WING

☐ C.A.P. BLAZER PATCH

☐ C.A.P. AIR SEARCH & RESCUE

☐ CIVIL AIR PATROL GUARD

☐ C.A.P. BLAZER PATCH

☐ STATION GUARD

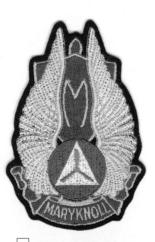
☐ C.A.P. MARYKNOLL

☐ BROOMFIELD SQDN.

☐ CADET SQUADRON
"NORTH DADE"
FLORIDA

CIVILIAN UNITS

☐ HIGH SCHOOL
VICTORY CORPS,
PRODUCTION

☐ HIGH SCHOOL
VICTORY CORPS,
AVIATION

☐ HIGH SCHOOL
VICTORY CORPS,
SEA

☐ HIGH SCHOOL
VICTORY CORPS,
LAND

☐ HIGH SCHOOL
VICTORY CORPS,
COMMUNITY

☐ HIGH SCHOOL
VICTORY CORPS

☐ CIVIL DEFENSE
CORPS

☐ CIVIL DEFENSE

☐ CIVIL DEFENSE
AUXILIARY POLICE

☐ CIVIL DEFENSE
ROAD REPAIR
CREW

☐ CIVIL DEFENSE
ELETRICAL REPAIR
CREW

☐ CIVIL DEFENSE
AIR RAID WARDEN

☐ CIVIL DEFENSE
BOMB SQUAD

☐ CIVIL DEFENSE
MESSENGER

☐ NON - COMBATANT
WAR AIDE

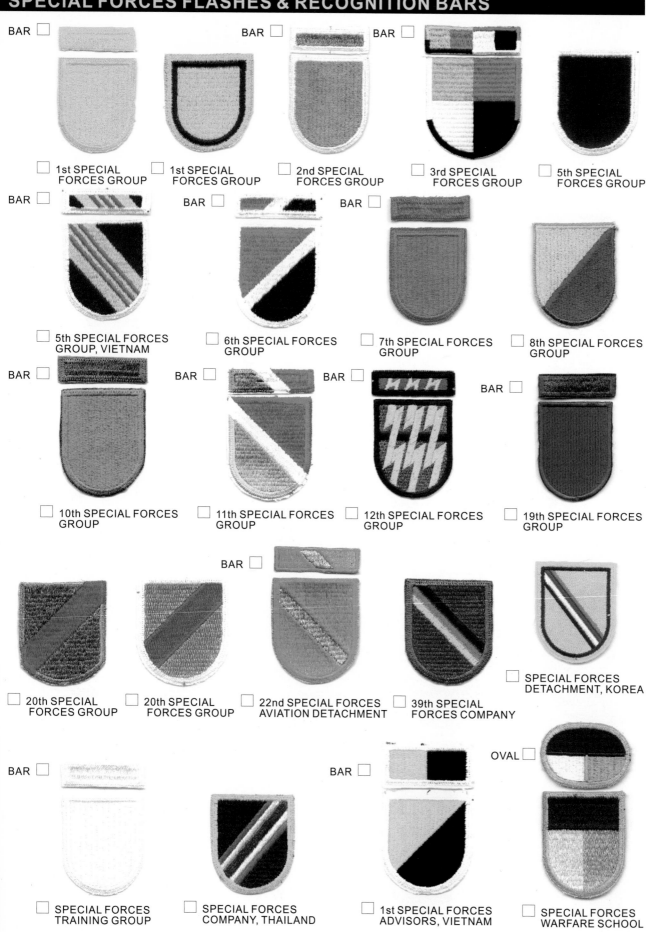

BAR ☐

BAR ☐

BAR ☐

☐ 1st SPECIAL FORCES GROUP

☐ 1st SPECIAL FORCES GROUP

☐ 2nd SPECIAL FORCES GROUP

☐ 3rd SPECIAL FORCES GROUP

☐ 5th SPECIAL FORCES GROUP

BAR ☐

BAR ☐

BAR ☐

☐ 5th SPECIAL FORCES GROUP, VIETNAM

☐ 6th SPECIAL FORCES GROUP

☐ 7th SPECIAL FORCES GROUP

☐ 8th SPECIAL FORCES GROUP

BAR ☐

BAR ☐

BAR ☐

BAR ☐

☐ 10th SPECIAL FORCES GROUP

☐ 11th SPECIAL FORCES GROUP

☐ 12th SPECIAL FORCES GROUP

☐ 19th SPECIAL FORCES GROUP

BAR ☐

☐ 20th SPECIAL FORCES GROUP

☐ 20th SPECIAL FORCES GROUP

☐ 22nd SPECIAL FORCES AVIATION DETACHMENT

☐ 39th SPECIAL FORCES COMPANY

☐ SPECIAL FORCES DETACHMENT, KOREA

BAR ☐

BAR ☐

OVAL ☐

☐ SPECIAL FORCES TRAINING GROUP

☐ SPECIAL FORCES COMPANY, THAILAND

☐ 1st SPECIAL FORCES ADVISORS, VIETNAM

☐ SPECIAL FORCES WARFARE SCHOOL

General Outline of Army Organization

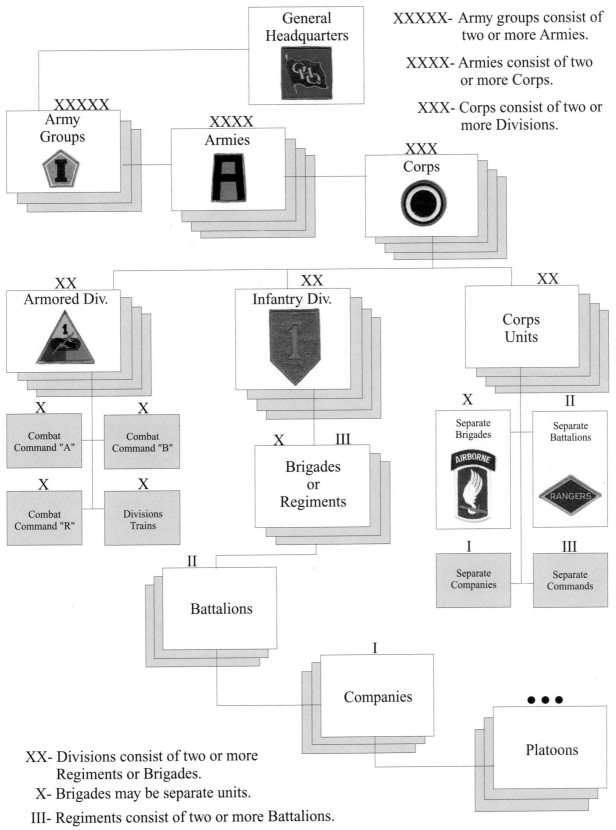

General Headquarters

XXXXX- Army groups consist of two or more Armies.

XXXX- Armies consist of two or more Corps.

XXX- Corps consist of two or more Divisions.

XXXXX
Army Groups

XXXX
Armies

XXX
Corps

XX
Armored Div.

XX
Infantry Div.

XX
Corps Units

X Combat Command "A"

X Combat Command "B"

X Combat Command "R"

X Divisions Trains

X III
Brigades or Regiments

X Separate Brigades — AIRBORNE

II Separate Battalions — RANGERS

I Separate Companies

III Separate Commands

II
Battalions

I
Companies

● ● ●
Platoons

XX- Divisions consist of two or more Regiments or Brigades.

X- Brigades may be separate units.

III- Regiments consist of two or more Battalions.

II- Battalions consist of two or more Companies.

I- Companies consist of two or more Platoons.

● ● ● - Platoons consist of two or more Squads.

● ● - Squads consist of nine individuals.

81

UNUSUAL FACTS ABOUT INTERESTING PATCHES
Reasons why some patches are designed the way they are.

Third Army

At the end of WW I, the US Third Army was assigned as "The Watch on the Rhine" in the Army of Occupation in Germany. When a request for a patch design was made, it was decided that they would incorporate the letters "A" and "O" (Army of Occupation) in the design along with the national colors of red, white and blue.

During the American Civil War, Corps in the Union army were indicated by a series of geometric shapes in order to simplify identification in battle. These shapes were usually cut from a piece of flannel and attached to the top of the kepi or to the front of the brimmed hat. The different divisions in the corps were indicated by the shape in different colors - red, white and blue for the First, Second and Third Divisions respectively. Some of these designs have survived to the present day in the forms of the I Corps and XXIV Corps

XXIV Corps

The Fourth Division uses a rebus as a basis for their design. The four leaves of ivy indicating the division number and the Roman numeral IV. Pronounced "I-V".

4th Division

The Fifth Division has a red diamond which was originally used as a baggage and vehicle marker during WW I.

The Seventh Division has 2 "7s" - one in the regular position and the other inverted making the familiar hourglass design.

27th Division

The 27th Division uses a pun on the name of its' commander, MG O'Ryan, by making the stars in the patch form the constellation Orion.

Since the 28th Division was formed with men from Pennsylvania, the keystone, which is the state symbol, was adopted for their design.

The 38th "Cyclone" division was so named because while in training in Mississippi during WW I, a storm leveled the units encampment They promptly adopted the motto and used the letters CY to indicate the name.

38th Division

When America entered WW I, the War Department wanted a division made up of National Guard troops from many states to fight in France. The 42nd Division was formed with men from 26 states and the District of Columbia and was called the "Rainbow" division because of the variety of origins of the troop.

Perhaps the best known example of a division changing designs for political correctness belongs

45th Division
(OLD)   (NEW)

to the 45th Division. From its' beginnings as an Arizona, New Mexico, Oklahoma and Colorado National Guard division, they had used the ancient indian symbol of the swastika.   With the rise of the Nazis, this emblem fell into disrepute.   So, in 1939, the division changed from the swastika to the more popular Indian symbol of the Thunderbird.

The 82th Division patch is based on the red square and blue circle used to mark the baggage and vehicles during WW I.   When troops were added from six widely separated army posts , the name "All American" was coined and the initials "AA" were added to the insignia.   It became an Airborne division in 1942.

Since most of the troops in the 83rd Division during WW I were from Ohio, the patch design is an anagram of the letters O-H-I-O.

Originally called the "Texas and Oklahoma' Division, during WW I the 90th was composed of troops primarily from the two states.   Therefore, the initials "T and O' in the patch design.

The 92nd Division patch design and name originated from the fact that the Indians called the Negro soldiers "Black Buffalos" when the troops dressed in the heavy buffalo robes in winter.

102d Division

Because most of the troops constituting the organization came from Missouri and Arkansas, an ingenious use of both an anagram and a rebus in patch design is the 102d "Ozark" Division.   When worn correctly, the letters "O" and "Z" are quite apparent and under the "Z" is an arc. Thereby : O+Z+Arc = OZARK.

1st SSF

THE FIRST SPECIAL SERVICE FORCE -

This unique international organization consisted of troops from both Canada and the U.S. who originally were destined for winter operations behind enemy lines. The patch used the words "USA" and CANADA" in white on a red arrowhead and was worn by both U.S. and Canadian troops.

Originally, the allied planners in WW II made provisions for the invasion and liberation of Norway. To this end the 99th Infantry Battalion (Separate) was formed in 1942. The concept was to enlist only Norwegian nationals. After mountain training at

99th Inf. Bn. (SEP)

Camp Hale, Colorado the battalion was sent to England and finished the war fighting on the continent. The patch design was that of a Viking sailing ship which indicated the units native background. The colors, red, white and blue are the same for both the U.S. and Norway. When the 99th Infantry Battalion and the First Special Service Force (which included former Rangers) were inactivated, the 474th Infantry Regiment was born, which later became

74th Regt. Combat Team

the 74th Regimental Combat Team. This new unit was designated to go to Norway to assist in the immediate post-hostilities repatriation of Axis forces.   The patch was a composite of the red arrowhead from the first SSF, the Viking ship from the 99th and the Ranger scroll. This patch is also encountered with a blue arrowhead. There is no evidence that this was ever authorized so it exists as a novelty and was quite possibly a manufacturers' error.

ORGANIZATON OF U.S. ARMY INFANTRY DIVISIONS OF WORLD WAR II

INFANTRY DIVISION	INFANTRY REGIMENTS			DIVISIONAL OR FIELD ARTY.				ENGR BTN.	RECON TRP.	MED. BTN.	SIG. CO.	ORD. CO.	Q.M. CO.	C.I.C. DTC.
1st "Big Red One"	16	18	26	5	7	32	33	1	1	1	1	701	1	1
2nd "Indian Head"	9	23	38	12	15	37	38	2	2	2	2	702	2	2
3rd "Rock of the Marne"	7	15	309	10	39	41	10	3	3	3	3	703	3	3
4th "Ivy Division"	8	12	22	20	29	42	44	4	4	4	4	704	4	4
5th "Red Diamond"	2	10	11	19	21	46	50	7	5	5	5	705	5	5
6th "Sight Seein' Sixth"	1	20	63	1	51	53	80	6	6	6	6	706	6	6
7th "Bayonet"	17	32	184	31	48	51	53	13	7	7	7	707	7	7
8th "Pathfinders"	13	28	121	28	43	45	56	12	8	8	8	708	8	8
9th "Octofoil"	39	47	60	26	34	60	84	15	9	9	9	709	9	9
10th "Mountain"	85	86	87	604	605	616	-	126	10	10	110	710	10	10
11th Airborne	187	188	511	457	472	674	675	127	-	221	511	711	408	-
13th Airborne	326	515	517	458	460	676	677	129	-	222	513	713	409	-
17th Airborne	194	507	513	464	466	680	681	139	-	224	517	717	411	-
23rd "America"	132	164	182	245	245	247	221	57	21	121	26	721	125	182
24th "Victory"	19	21	34	11	13	52	63	3	24	24	24	724	24	24
25th "Tropic Lightning"	27	35	161	8	64	89	90	65	25	25	25	725	25	25
26th "Yankee"	101	104	328	101	102	180	263	101	26	114	39	726	26	26
27th "New York"	105	106	165	104	105	106	249	102	27	102	27	727	27	27
28th "Keystone"	109	110	112	107	108	109	229	103	28	103	28	728	28	28
29th "Blue & Gray"	115	116	175	110	111	224	227	121	29	104	29	729	29	29
30th "Old Hickory"	117	119	120	113	118	197	230	105	30	105	30	730	30	30
31st "Dixie"	124	155	167	114	116	117	149	106	31	106	31	731	31	31
32nd "Red Arrow"	126	127	128	120	121	126	129	114	32	107	32	732	32	32
33rd "Illinois"	123	130	136	122	123	124	210	108	33	108	33	733	33	33
34th "Red Bull"	133	135	168	125	151	175	185	109	34	109	34	734	34	34
35th "Santa Fe"	134	137	320	127	161	216	219	60	35	110	35	735	35	35

INFANTRY DIVISION	INFANTRY REGIMENTS			DIVISIONAL OR FIELD ARTY BNS.				ENGR BN.	RECON TRP.	MED BN.	SIG CO.	ORD CO.	Q.M. CO.	C.I.C. DET.
36th "Texas"	141	142	143	131	132	133		155	111	36	111	36	736	36
37th "Buckeye"	129	145	148	6	135	136		140	117	37	112	37	737	37
38th "Cyclone"	149	151	152	138	139	150		163	113	38	113	38	738	38
39th "Delta"				- This division was not activated during WW II -										
40th "Sunshine"	108	160	185	143	164	213		222	115	40	115	40	740	40
41st "Sunset"	162	163	186	146	167	205		218	116	41	116	41	741	41
42nd "Rainbow"	222	232	242	232	292	402		542	142	42	122	42	742	42
43rd "Winged Victory"	103	169	172	103	152	169		192	118	43	118	43	743	43
44th Division	71	114	324	156	157	217		220	63	44	119	44	744	44
45th "Thunderbird"	157	179	180	158	160	171		189	120	45	120	45	700	45
63rd "Blood & Fire"	253	254	255	718	861	862		863	263	63	363	563	763	63
65th "Battle-axe"	259	260	261	720	867	868		869	265	65	365	565	765	65
66th "Black Panther"	262	263	264	721	870	871		872	266	66	366	566	766	66
69th "Fighting 69th"	271	272	273	724	879	880		881	269	69	369	569	769	69
70th "Trailblazers"	274	275	276	725	882	883		884	270	70	370	570	770	70
71st "Red Circle"	5	14	66	564	607	608		609	271	71	371	571	771	251
75th Division	289	290	291	730	897	898		899	275	75	375	575	775	75
76th "Onaway"	304	385	417	302	355	364		901	301	76	301	76	776	76
77th "Statue of Liberty"	305	306	307	304	305	306		902	302	77	302	77	777	77
78th "Lightning"	309	310	311	307	308	309		903	303	78	303	78	778	78
79th "Cross of Lorraine"	313	314	315	310	311	312		904	304	79	304	79	779	79
80th "Blue Ridge"	317	318	319	313	314	315		905	305	80	305	80	780	80
81st "Wildcat"	321	322	323	316	317	318		906	306	81	306	81	781	81
82nd "All American"	325	504	505	319	320	376		456	307	82	307	82	782	-
83rd "Thunderbolt"	329	330	331	322	323	324		908	308	83	308	83	783	83
84th "Railsplitters"	333	334	335	325	326	327		909	309	84	309	84	784	84
85th "Custer"	337	338	339	328	329	403		910	310	85	310	85	785	85

INFANTRY DIVISIONS	INFANTRY REGIMENTS			DIVISIONAL OR FIELD ARTY BNS.				ENGR. BN.	RECON. TRPS.	MED. BN.	SIG. CO.	ORD. CO.	Q.M. CO.	C.I.C. DET.
86th "Blackhawk"	341	342	343	331	332	404	911	311	86	311	86	786	86	86
87th "Golden Acorn"	345	346	347	334	335	336	912	312	87	312	87	787	87	87
88th "Blue Devil"	349	350	351	337	338	339	913	313	88	313	88	788	88	88
89th "Rolling W"	353	354	355	340	341	563	914	314	89	314	89	789	405	89
90th "Tough Ombres"	357	358	359	343	344	345	915	315	90	315	90	790	90	90
91st "Powder River"	361	362	363	346	347	348	916	316	91	316	91	791	91	91
92nd "Buffalo"	365	370	371	597	598	599	600	317	92	317	92	792	92	92
93rd Division	25	368	369	593	594	595	596	318	93	318	93	793	93	93
94th "Neuf-Cats"	301	302	376	301	356	390	919	319	94	319	94	794	94	94
95th "Victory"	377	378	379	358	359	360	920	320	95	320	95	795	95	95
96th "Deadeye"	381	382	383	361	362	363	921	321	96	321	96	796	96	96
97th "Trident"	303	386	387	303	365	389	922	322	97	322	97	797	97	97
98th "Iriquois"	389	390	391	367	368	399	923	323	98	323	98	798	98	98
99th "Checkerboard"	393	394	395	370	371	372	924	324	99	324	99	799	99	99
100th "Century"	397	398	399	373	374	375	925	325	100	325	100	800	100	100
101st "Screaming Eagles"	327	401	502	321	377	463	907	326	-	326	101	801	426	101
102nd "Ozark"	405	406	407	379	380	381	927	327	102	327	102	802	102	102
103rd "Cactus"	409	410	411	382	383	384	928	328	103	328	103	803	103	103
104th "Timberwolf"	413	414	415	385	386	387	929	329	104	329	104	804	104	104
106th "Golden Lion"	422	423	424	589	592	591	592	81	106	331	106	806	106	106
1st Allied Abn Task Fce	517	509	550	460	463	602	-	596	-	676	512	-	334	-

GLOSSARY

AAA — Anti-Aircraft Artillery
AAF — Army Air Force
AF — Air Force
A/B — Airborne
ACR — Armored Cavalry Regiment
Admin. — Administration
AFCE — Allied Forces Central Euro0pe
AGF — Army Ground Forces
ARCOM — Army Reserve Command
Arrmd. — Armored
ARVN — Army of the Republic of Vietnam
Arty. — Artillery
ASF — Army Service Forces
Aslt. — Assault
A.S.T.P. — Army Specialized Training Program
Bde. — Brigade
Bn. — Battalion
CA — Coast Artillery
CAP — Civil Air Patro
Cav. — Cavalry
Chem. — Chemical
Cmbt. — Combat
Cmd. — Command
Cmdr. — Commander
Co. — Company
Comm. — Communications
Ctr. — Center
Def. — Defense
Dept. — Department
Disp. — Dispensary
Dist. — District
Div. — Division
DMZ — Demilitarized Zone
DUKW — Amphibious tracked vehicle
Engr. — Engineer
ETO — European Theatre of Operations
Evac. — Evacuation
F.A. — Field Artillery
Fld. Arty. — Field Artillery
FMF-PAC — Fleet Marine Force-Pacific
GHQ — General Headquarters
Gov. — Government
Gp. — Group
Grp. — Group
H/C — Hardcore
H & H — Headquarters & Headquarters Company
Heli. — Helicopter
HHC — Headquarters & Headquarters Company
Hqs. — Headquarters
Inf. — Infantry
Intel. — Intelligence
Instr. — Instructor
KMAG — Korean Military Assistance Group
Log. — Logisstical
LRRP — Long Range Reconnaissance Patrol
MAAG — Military Assistance Advisory Group
M.A.C. — Marine Amphibious Command
MAC-V — Military Assistance Command - Vietnaml
Maint. — Maintenance
Mech. — Mechanized
Med. — Medical
Mgt. — Management
M.I. — Military Intelligence
Mil. — Military
MLM — Military Liason Mission
M.P — Military Police

NAV/SWG. — Naval Special Warfare Group
NCO — Non-Commissioned Officer
NCOA — Non-Commissioned Officer Academy
N.E. — North East
N.W. — North West
OCS — Officer Candidate School
ODA — Operational Detachment "A"
OPFOR — Opposing Forces
Ord — Ordnance
OSS — Office of Strategic Services
Pers. — Personnel
Q.M. — Quartermaster
Plt. — Platoon
Pol. — Police
RCT — Regimental Combat Team
R & D — Research & Development
Recon. — Reconnaissance
Regt. — Regiment
Rgt. — Regiment
ROTC — Reserve Officers Training Corps
SCARWAF — Special Category Army With Air Force
Sch. — School
Sect. — Section
S.E. — South East
SETAF — Southern European Task Force
SMC — Armored Corps - Unidentified
Sqdn. — Squadron
SHAEF — Supreme HQ Allied Expeditionary Forces
SOG — Special Operations Group
Spec. — Specialist
Spt. — Support
Sub. — Subdued
S.W. — South Wes
Sys. — System
TM — Training Manual
Trans. — Transportation
Trng. — Training
U.S. — United States
USAAF — U.S. Army Air Force
USAF — U.S. Air Force
VN — Vietnam
WAAC — Women's Auxiliary Army Corps
WW I — World War I
WW II — World War II

Bibliography

American Society of Military Insignia Collectors; *The Trading Post;* Published quarterly by the society. Membership information may be obtained from Scott Hughes; 3415 Tilley Morris Road; Matthews, NC 28105-7121.

Barker, Geoffrey T.; *A Concise History of U.S. Army Special Operations Forces, Volume one, 2nd Edition;* Anglo-American Publishing Co., Tampa, FL; 1988 & 1993.

Barker, Geoffrey T.; *A Concise History of the U.S. Airborne Army, Corps, Divisions and Brigades;* Anglo-American Publishing Co., Tampa, FL; 1989.

Barker, Geoffrey T.; *A Concise History of the U.S. Army Airborne Infantry;* Anglo-American Publishing Co., Tampa, FL, 1989.

Baudouin, Ourari; *Badges and Uniforms of the World's Elite Forces;* B&P Military Publications; Brussels, Belgium. 1984

Britton, Jack & George Washington, Jr.; *U. S. Military Shoulder Patches, Fifth Edition;* MCN Press, Tulsa, OK; 1990.

Insignia and Decorations of the U.S. Armed Forces; National Geographic Society, Washington, DC; 1945

Johnson, Lawrence H. III; *Winged Sabers;* Stackpole Books, Harrisburg, PA, 1990.

LIFE Magazine; August 6, 1945, pp 40-46.

McDuff, James M.; *U.S. Army Shoulder Sleeve Insignia of the Vietnam War;* Published by the author; 1982.

Smith, Richard W. & Roy A. Pelz; *Shoulder Sleeve Insignia of the U. S. Armed Forces, 1941-1945;* Richard W. Smith, Hendersonville, TN; 1981.

Smith, Richard W. & Roy A. Pelz; *Shoulder Sleeve Insignia of the U. S. Army, 1946-1976;* University of Evansville Press, Evansville, IN, 1978.

Stanton, Shelby L.; *Vietnam Order of Battle;* US News Books, Washington, DC; 1981.

Stanton, Shelby L.; *Order of Battle, U.S. Army World War II;* Presidio Press, Novato, CA; 1984.

Whittaker, Len; *Some Talk of Private Armies;* Albanium Publishing Co., Harpenden, Herts. UK, 1984.

Thompson, Leoy; *Badges and Insignia of the Elite Forces;* Arms & Armour Press, London, UK. 1991.

Sutherland, LTC Ian D.W.; *Special Forces of the United States Army;* R. James Bender Publishing, San Jose, CA 1990.